Introduction

In 1949 and 1950 when the *Himalaya* and the slightly smaller *Chusan* entered service with P&O, it was a sure sign that the company was getting back into its stride after the long years of disruption during, and immediately following, the Second World War. Resplendent in their white livery the two ships continued the tradition which had been started with the *Straths* almost 20 years previously, but the two new liners seemed somehow to have more individuality, and they were an instant success with the travelling public. Over the next 20 years, as Britain withdrew from Empire and the pattern of trade changed, the two ships retained their popularity and in the late 1950s, with the introduction of services into the Pacific Ocean, they became familiar and well loved ships in the West Coast ports of the USA.

In the early 1970s the two vessels were withdrawn from service and sold to the scrapyards of Taiwan, having fallen victim to the combined pressures of commercial competition from wide-bodied jet airliners, the politics and war in the Middle East which closed the Suez Canal and generated dramatic increases in the price of fuel, and the appearance on the scene of purpose-built cruise ships. However, right to the end they remained popular with the ship's companies who manned them and with the passengers who travelled in them, and this book is a tribute to two magnificent British passenger liners.

Neil McCart
Cheltenham
April 1996

To Caroline & Louise

Jacket illustrations courtesy of P&O & Don Smith

Jacket Design: Louise McCart
© Neil McCart/FAN PUBLICATIONS 1996
ISBN: 0 9519538 7 7

Typesetting By: Highlight Type Bureau Ltd, Clifton House, 2 Clifton Villas, Bradford, West Yorkshire BD8 7BY

Printing By: The Amadeus Press Ltd, 517 Leeds Road, Huddersfield, West Yorkshire HD2 1YJ

Famous British Liners

P&O's Himalaya & Chusan – Rebuilding The Fleet

by Neil McCart

Contents

D1464474

Published By FAN PUBLICATIONS
17 Wymans Lane, Cheltenham, GL51 9QA, England. Fax & Tel 01242 580290

Chapter One

The Dawn Of A New Era

When the Second World War finally ended on 2 September 1945, Britain was virtually bankrupt as a result of crippling war debts. The end of the war marked the beginning of the country's economic problems, with debts of almost £3,000 million, and with the cutting off of American aid, the Treasury warned of a 'Financial Dunkirk'. On top of this the country had lost 30 per cent of its merchant fleet, and one of the companies which had suffered the most was the Peninsular & Oriental Steam Navigation Company. During the years of war P&O had lost six of its large passenger ships through enemy action, one as a result of a fire and one which had been purchased by the Admiralty for use as a fleet repair ship. Included in these losses was the magnificent *Viceroy of India* which was only 12 years old, and the newest ship in its passenger fleet, the four-year-old *Strathallan*.

Despite the crippling war debts the British government still had to maintain its overseas empire along with huge garrisons of troops, particularly in the Middle East and India. In order to do this they also needed to retain many of the passenger liners which they had requisitioned during the early months of the war, and it was clear that normal passenger and cargo routes would not see a return to scheduled peacetime services for some time.

It was under these uncertain conditions that, in January 1946, P&O placed an order with Vickers Armstrong Ltd of Barrow-in-Furness for a new 28,000-ton passenger ship for its Australian service. Four months later they placed a second order with the same shipbuilder, this time for a 24,000-ton passenger vessel for the Far Eastern service. Not only were these valuable orders for Vickers Armstrong, but the P&O Company were also demonstrating great faith in a recovery which was by no means a foregone conclusion.

On 29 April 1946, just three months after the order had been placed, the first keel plates were laid for job number 951 which would eventually become the *Himalaya*. Originally delivery of the ship was set for January 1948, but with shortages of steel and skilled labour, coupled with delays in the supply of essential fittings, it was apparent that there were going to be many set-backs before the vessel was finally ready. Another sign of those difficult times was the increase in costs. In Janaury 1946 when the liner was ordered, the estimated cost of building was put at £2,244,000, but, in fact, the final figure turned out to be £3,500,000, an increase of £1,256,000. The costs of shipbuilding were more than two and a half times the pre-war prices and it was obvious that post-war reconstruction could not match that which had followed the 1914-18 war.

The launch of the *Himalaya* on Tuesday 5 October 1948.

(Sankey Collection)

28 June 1949, and the *Himalaya* and the *Chusan* are together alongside the fitting-out basin at Vickers' shipyard. Work on the former ship is almost completed, while the latter has just been towed round to the berth following her launch. *(VSEL)*

It had been intended that the keel for the second liner would be laid during the autumn of 1946, but in the event there was no berth available and it was February 1947 before the keel for yard number 967, the *Chusan*, was laid. The same problems of shortages and delays affected the second vessel and there were further complications when, in late 1948, the stem of the partially built ship had to be cut away in the shape of an arc. The reason for this unusual event was that one of the builder's light railways passed the head of the berth and the removal of the stem was necessary in order to allow engines and laden trucks to pass freely. Fortunately Vickers were in the process of spending over £1 million to move the line, and once the track had been relaid in a new position away from the construction berth, the missing portion of the *Chusan's* stem was welded back into position.

Meanwhile, work was progressing well on the *Himalaya* and on Tuesday 5 October 1948 hull number 951 was launched. Large crowds gathered, as was usual in those days when a launching ceremony meant a gala day for the whole town, and the event was recorded by a newsreel camera team and by Press representatives from all over the Commonwealth. The ceremony took place at 12.43pm, as Lady Currie, the wife of the P&O chairman, caused the traditional bottle of wine to smash against the raked stem of the new vessel while she pronounced the equally traditional good wishes for the ship. Then slowly at first, but with gathering speed, the great hull slid into the waters of the

Walney Channel; waiting tugs hooted a welcome, the crowds cheered and the shipyard band played. The only unexpected event of the day occurred when one of the waiting tugs went aground and had to be towed free by one of the others before it could assist in towing the *Himalaya* into the Buccleuch Dock for fitting out. Two days later it was announced that the *Himalaya's* first master would be Captain D. M. Stuart DSO, the commodore of the P&O fleet. After completing his apprenticeship Captain Stuart had joined the P&O Company in June 1909 and had served in many of the company's vesels. He had been in command of the *Cathay* when she was sunk by an enemy air attack at Bougie in November 1942, and subsequently he had commanded the *Ranchi*, *Canton*, *Strathaird* and *Strathmore*.

Following the launching ceremony work continued on the *Himalaya's* fitting out and by the second half of August 1949 she was ready for sea. On Sunday 21 August Vickers opened her to the public and such was the interest in her that special trains were laid on from Lancaster to cater for the numbers travelling to Barrow to view the new ship. Despite the fact that the country was in the middle of a heat wave, some visitors waited for up to four hours in long queues which extended from the ship right through the shipyard to Kings Gate, along Michaelson Road, down the full length of the Buccleuch Dock Road and then back to Michaelson Road. It was past 7pm before the Kings Gate could be closed and even then the long queue within the yard had to make its slow progress to the ship before touring the vessel. In all 20,000 people visited the *Himalaya* that day, which gives some idea of the interest generated. During her remaining three nights at Barrow the *Himalaya* provided a magnificent spectacle with her illuminated superstructure and funnel dominating the shipyard, a sight which drew crowds of spectators to the nearby high level bridge.

Tuesday 23 August 1949 dawned sunny and bright and by 11am, when the *Himalaya* cast off from her berth in Ramsden Dock, the south end of Walney Island and Roa and Piel Islands were crowded with well wishers. The best part of an hour was spent manoeuvring her out of the dock and into the channel, and it was gone midday before the *Himalaya*, escorted by two tugs, rounded Roa Island where, in response to the cheers of the crowds, Captain Stuart bade farewell to Barrow on the ship's loudspeaker system. By 12.30pm the *Himalaya* had disappeared into the prevailing haze as courses were set for Belfast where she arrived early the next morning to be dry docked before carrying out her trials on the Clyde.

The *Himalaya* left Belfast in the early hours of Saturday 27 August 1949 and later that day she anchored off Greenock where her acceptance trials were to take place. Over the following two days the ship was put through her paces, and on the measured mile she attained speeds of 25.13 knots before, in the early evening of Monday 29 August, she returned to her Clyde anchorage where nearly 400 special guests were embarked for the voyage south to Southampton. The liner left the Firth of Clyde after dark, and with her funnel brilliantly lit and her name displayed in neon strips at the base of it, she looked a magnificent sight. During the journey the ship's consumption trials were carried out and, with passengers and Press representatives embarked, the hotel services could be put through their paces. Geoffrey Hilton, who was a member of the ship's company, recalls an amusing incident which took place on the day after the ship left Greenock: 'One of the special passengers, a very dear old lady, who was obviously a well-travelled person, stopped one of the ship's senior officers on the boat deck and enquired whether the speed trials had been successful. "Yes, Madam, very successful", replied the officer. "We achieved a speed of 25.13 knots over the measured mile." Whereupon this elderly but observant passenger remarked, "Isn't that absolutely marvellous, and with only one funnel too!" One could visualize this dear old soul treading the decks of Victorian and Edwardian three- and four-funnelled liners and making similar observations.'

Daybreak on Tuesday saw the ship off the Welsh coast and by midday she was off Lands End, entering the Channel soon afterwards. However, when she was off Start Point she encountered her first thick fog and with visibility down to less than 100 yards, speed was reduced to eight knots. This reduction in speed also brought her consumption trials to a temporary halt until the ship was turned round and steamed west of the Isles of Scilly where the trials were resumed. During the afternoon of Wednesday 31 August 1949, with her trials successfully completed, the liner entered the Solent

Himalaya leaves the shipbuilder's yard on the morning of Tuesday 23 August 1949 for dry docking at Belfast and her trials on the Clyde.
(Sankey Collection)

The *Himalaya* makes a splendid sight as she runs her speed trials off Arran at the end of August 1949. She is still flying the builder's house-flag as she was formally handed over to P&O at Southampton on 1 September 1949. *(P&O)*

On Saturday 6 June 1950 the *Chusan* left the Barrow shipyard of Vickers Armstrong bound for Liverpool, and then the Clyde for her trials.
(Sankey Collection)

and anchored for the night in Cowes Roads, where she was again the centre of attention. Early next morning she weighed anchor and entered Southampton Water for the final stage of her voyage, and by mid-morning she was alongside 30-31 berths at the mouth of the River Itchen in the city's Eastern Docks. Soon after her arrival, as crowds gathered on the shore at Woolston to see the new ship, the *Himalaya* was formally handed over to her owners by the builders, Vickers Armstrong. Following the signing of the formal documentation by Sir William Currie and a director of Vickers Armstrong, the ship's officers paraded on the fore deck and saluted as the builder's flag was lowered and the P&O house-flag was broken at the mast-head.

Meanwhile, back at Barrow, work continued on the *Chusan*, and in the early afternoon of Tuesday 28 June 1949 she too took to the waters of the Walney Channel. The naming ceremony was performed by the Viscountess Bruce, wife of the Viscount Bruce of Melbourne, a former Prime Minister of Australia and a director of the P&O Company. Once again all the glamour of a launching day was there, the large crowds, the Barrow shipyard band playing lively music and, of course, the massive, gleaming white hull of the *Chusan* which made an impressive picture as it stood out

against the cranes at the launching berths. At just after 1pm the ceremony got under way when Viscountess Bruce named the ship and wished her 'good luck', then pressed the lever which released the traditional bottle of wine. The new liner was sent down the slipway as the shipyard band played 'Eternal Father', and the thousands of spectators held their breath for ten long seconds as the *Chusan* rolled precariously to starboard just as she entered the water. Then there was a great sigh of relief all round as she righted herself and rocked gently to and fro in the water. In fact the launching cradle on the starboard bow had broken as the vessel ran down to the water, and as she listed, the men lining her rails had run to the other side of the deck. Afterwards Viscountess Bruce was heard to comment, 'I understood that it is normal for a ship to curtsey, but this one waved to me.'

Fortunately, the ship had not sustained any damage and six tugs towed her into the Buccleuch Dock, where she was moored astern of the almost completed *Himalaya* for work on the fitting out to begin. One advantage which was a direct result of the delays in delivering the *Chusan*, was the fact that the vessel could be fitted with the newly developed Denny-Brown 'hydrofin automatic stabilizers' which had been manufactured by Brown Brothers & Co Ltd of Edinburgh, in

The *Chusan* at speed in the Firth of Clyde.   *(VSEL)*

conjunction with William Denny & Brothers Ltd of Dumbarton. The equipment was fitted in a watertight compartment which was situated forward of the boiler-room, aft of the refrigeration machinery, and beneath the fuel-oil deep tanks. The stabilizers themselves consisted of two retractable and rotatable fins of rectangular plan form and an aerofoil section arranged in a horizontal plane at either side of the ship. In operation, each fin was tilted from the zero position, first in one direction and then in the other, with the movement of the port and starboard fins being controlled in such a way that their angular displacements were equal and opposite. With the forward motion of the ship, the water exerted an upward force on one fin and a downward force on the other, thus counteracting the actions of the sea. The orientation of the fins was controlled by gyroscopic equipment and the hydraulic machinery was controlled from the bridge. The *Chusan* was, in fact, the first British passenger liner to be fitted with Denny-Brown stabilizers.

By the spring of 1950 work on the *Chusan* was nearing completion, and in addition to a summer cruise programme to the Atlantic Isles and into the Mediterranean, an extra nine-day cruise from Southampton on 1 July to Madeira and Lisbon, carrying only first class passengers, was included in her schedule. With fares for the cruise starting at £25 it was fully booked, as were all the other summer cruises.

In April 1950 the main body of the ship's company began to join the liner and one of those who received instructions to join the *Chusan* was Richard Firth, who was to be the Junior Second Officer. He recalls events of those days: 'Before joining the *Chusan* I was ordered to Southampton to meet the Royal Mail Line's MV *Alcantara*, where I joined up with Bill

Vickers and a senior steward to muster the Asian crew members who had arrived from Bombay. We were allocated a special train from Southampton to Barrow-in-Furness and, to put it mildly, the rolling stock was vintage. The first class compartment which had been set aside for Bill and myself was definitely Victorian; with hard, upright seats and solid wooden arm rests it was most uncomfortable and there was no chance of a "kip" *en route*. We pulled out of Southampton Station during the afternoon of 1 June and the train then seemed to meander round the countryside of southern England for a very long time before we finally stopped at Cheltenham for a belated tea break. Unfortunately the tea and buns were on the wrong platform, but we found a crossing and trundled all the urns and trays over to the train. However, having spent the best part of an hour making sure that all 200 of the Indian crew were sustained, there was nothing left for we three Europeans. Fortunately a very helpful Station Master said he would telephone Birmingham and get them to arrange something for us. Sure enough, he was as good as his word, and when we finally arrived in Birmingham a very old-fashioned, liveried gentleman brought three packs of sandwiches and tea on a silver salver. He then proceeded, very formally, to lay a napkin on each of our knees before he left us with our refreshments. It was dark when we left Birmingham and the train then trundled through the night and arrived at Vickers' at 5am the following morning. We were met by a not too happy Chief Officer, Gerry Randall, who had been up for most of the night awaiting our arrival. Once on board there was very little time to find one's way around for, on Saturday 3 June 1950, we left Barrow bound for Liverpool and then the Clyde where our trials were to take place.'

After spending three days in Liverpool the *Chusan* steamed north for the Firth of Clyde on Tuesday 6 June and for the rest of the week she underwent her trials. Richard Firth remembers the full power trials and the testing of the stabilizers: 'It was a gloriously calm day with yachts and pleasure boats everywhere when we roared through them all at over 23 knots then, after a rerun, all hell was let loose. The Vickers' "boffins" and Captain Robert Tunbridge agreed that "these things", as he called the stabilizers, should be put through their paces and the only way this could be done on a flat calm sea was to activate them in reverse while steaming at a fast speed down the Clyde. This was duly done and the *Chusan* started to roll at angles of up to 17° to port and starboard. The sight of this massive ship wallowing around on the glassy calm of the Clyde sent all the yachts and pleasure boats scattering. Unfortunately, in the dining saloon, where the stewards had just laid up all the tables, the extent of the rolling took everyone by surprise and quite a lot of crockery was lost. On a personal note I always preferred the motion of a rolling ship without stabilizers.'

Shortly before leaving the Clyde during the evening of Monday 12 June, guests of the company and representatives of the Press were embarked for the voyage to Southampton, during which fuel consumption trials were also carried out. The *Chusan* arrived off the Isle of Wight during the morning of Wednesday 14 June, and here the stabilizers were tested once again. The ship was made to keel over to both port and starboard in quick succession when steaming at 19 knots, and then she was instantaneously brought back to an even keel. However, this time, all on board were warned four times over the loudspeaker to ensure that all movable articles were safely secured.

On her arrival at Southampton that same afternoon ownership of the *Chusan* was transferred from the builders to the P&O Company, with Mr J. Reid-Young, a director, signing the documents on behalf of Vickers Armstrong Ltd, and Mr A. O. Laing, the deputy chairman of P&O, representing the shipping company. There then followed a short ceremony which was attended by the ship's company, when the builder's flag was hauled down and the P&O flag was hoisted at the mast-head.

With its two new ships in service this was the dawn of a new era for P&O.

P. & O. HIMALAYA - 1st CLASS SPORTS DECK

The *Himalaya's* first class sports area was on the Boat Deck. It was enclosed at both sides by folding glazed screens.

(Author's collection)

Chapter Two

Built For Comfort

The *Himalaya* and *Chusan* were the sixth and seventh large passenger liners to be built for P&O by Vickers Armstrong Ltd, and in the late 1940s and early 1950s they shared, with the Orient Line vessel *Orcades*, the distinction of being the largest and fastest passenger liners trading east of Suez. Both ships continued a close association between the builders and owners which had begun with the five *Strath* - class vessels in the 1930s and, in fact, they had a very similar hull form to the earlier ships. Not only were they from the same 'mould', but their profiles were not dissimilar to the popular *Straths*. They had a dignified and elegant appearance which was characterized by a raked stem, cruiser stern, lofty superstructure which was well rounded forward, and a single funnel. The main distinguishing feature was the fact that whereas the *Himalaya* had only one mast and three sets of derrick posts, the *Chusan* was fitted with two masts and two sets of derrick posts.

The *Himalaya*, which was intended for the busier and longer route between London and Sydney, had accommodation for 762 first class and 401 tourist class passengers. The numbers are an indication that, in the mid-1940s when she was designed, the mass emigration from the UK to the antipodes was not foreseen. The passenger accommodation in both classes was commodious and comfortable and the public rooms were decorated in a restrained contemporary style which eliminated non-essentials, a trend which had been started in the early 1930s with the Orient Line vessel, *Orion*. Passengers in both the first and tourist classes were provided with large areas of open deck space, which was attained by giving special attention to the enclosure within the deckhouses of ventilation units and other fitments. The design of both ships was generally admired and one feature which was considered a particular success was the enclosed sun-trap abaft the bridge, in which no breeze was felt even when the ship was steaming at over 25 knots.

The first class passenger accommodation was arranged on six decks, the Boat and Promenade Decks, and A to D Decks. As recreation space the Boat Deck provided a large area including the portion abaft the bridge which was enclosed at the sides by folding glazed screens to form the sun-trap. Some idea of its size may be gathered from the fact that it was laid out with nine deck tennis courts and 28 quoit 'bull ring' pitches. Descending the staircases from the Boat Deck brought one onto the Promenade Deck and, although there was plenty of open-air space, it was generally shady, which provided a more restful retreat than the Boat Deck. Most of the first class public rooms were arranged on the Promenade Deck, including the children's playroom and playground which were forward of No 3 cargo hatch. Aft of the hatch was the main foyer and staircase, and the lounge. Doors at the after end of the lounge gave access to the Australia Room on the port side of the ship and to the library on the starboard side. The former provided an annexe to the main lounge with special facilities for letter writing and, as the P&O Company had been directly associated with Australia for almost 100 years, the room was decorated in a style which identified that important link. Representative features included panelling of Australian woods on the bulkheads, curtains and covers of materials which were designed, woven and printed in Sydney, and water-colour paintings of Australian scenes by the Australian artist J. S. Loxton of Melbourne. It was the first time that the company had identified a particular room so closely with a Commonwealth country. The library on the starboard side occupied a similar area to the Australia Room and both gave access to the after end of the deck and to the dancing space, the sides of which

P. & O. HIMALAYA · 1st CLASS LOUNGE

The main first class lounge in the *Himalaya* was on the Promenade Deck and this view looks aft. *(Author's collection)*

The *Himalaya's* Australia Room was aft of the main lounge, on the port side. The room was decorated to identify P&O's 100-year link with that country. *(Author's collection)*

The *Himalaya's* first class Verandah Café, which also served as the Smoking Room, was at the after end of the Promenade Deck, overlooking the swimming-pool. *(Author's collection)*

were enclosed with folding and sliding glazed screens, while the teak deck planking was laid out in a panel formation. Doors at the after end of the dancing space allowed access to the Verandah Café, which also served as the first class Smoking Room, and which was made particularly attractive by its careful planning and by the extent of its glass covered area. The annexe at the after end also served as an entrance and it looked down to the first class swimming-pool which was below on A Deck.

The stateroom and cabin accommodation for first class passengers was situated on A, B, C and D Decks, with the suites and de luxe staterooms amidships on B Deck. At the forward end of A Deck, adjoining the entrance foyer and main stairway, were a shop and the hairdressing salons. The after end of the A Deck deckhouse formed a café which overlooked the first class swimming-pool. The two suites and the four cabins de luxe, which were arranged on B Deck, were panelled in light woods and elegantly furnished. An elaborate telephone system was installed which connected all the first class cabins and public rooms. For those first class passengers who were interested in the company's history, there were two reminders of previous ships which had borne the same name. The ship's bell from the first steamship *Himalaya* of 1853 which had, in fact, spent most of her career as a troop transport, was displayed in the foyer at the entrance to the

first class lounge. The second reminder was an oil painting of the *Himalaya* of 1892, a vessel which had a distinguished career of 30 years before being broken up in 1922. The painting depicted the vessel in the Thames and it was hung in the main lounge on the Promenade Deck.

The first class dining saloon was situated amidships on D Deck, and was reached by way of the main staircase or by two lifts which served all the first class passenger decks. It was designed to seat 389 passengers at round and square tables for two, four and six diners.

The 401 tourist class passengers were accommodated aft on A to F Decks. The tourist class Games Deck was at the after end of A Deck, and as well as a swimming-pool there were facilities for deck tennis and quoits. Beneath, on B Deck, there was a promenade space and the tourist class dancing space which, like that in the first class, was fitted with folding glazed screens and doubled as a cinema. On C Deck there was more open-air promenade space, the Smoking Room, shop and children's playroom. Beneath the Smoking Room, on D Deck, there was the tourist class lounge and forward of this, but separated from it by 30 cabins, was the tourist class dining saloon which could seat 208 passengers at tables for two, four and eight. The tourist class passengers were accommodated in two- or four-berth cabins which were mainly situated on E and F Decks, and all the cabins were

P. & O. HIMALAYA - 1st CLASS DINING SALOON

The *Himalaya's* first class dining saloon on D Deck could seat 389 passengers. It was reached by way of the main staircase.

(Author's collection)

The *Himalaya's* tourist class sports deck was at the after end of A Deck and it housed the tourist class swimming-pool.
(Author's collection)

The *Himalaya's* tourist class dining saloon on D Deck was a spacious compartment which could accommodate 208 passengers at one sitting. *(Author's collection)*

Himalaya's tourist class lounge which was situated aft on D Deck.
(Author's collection)

fitted with wash-hand basins, a facility which had not always been available in pre-war days.

Of the ship's company of 631, the master and his officers were accommodated on two decks, directly beneath the navigating bridge. The Goan and European crew members had berths right forward on B to E Decks and the remainder of the Asian crew members were accommodated right aft on C, D and E Decks. The deckhouse at the after end of B Deck contained the ship's hospital, with both general and isolation wards, and at the forward end of the same deck there was further hospital accommodation, including an operating theatre.

The *Himalaya* was a twin-screw ship, with each propeller being driven by a set of geared turbines which were designed to develop 34,000 SHP in normal service, but were capable of sustained operation at an overload of 25 per cent, so that the maximum power available was 42,500 SHP. The corresponding propeller speeds were 130 and 140 rpm respectively and the main machinery installation was, at that time, the most powerful which had been manufactured for a merchant ship. The superheated steam was supplied to the turbines by four Foster Wheeler, controlled superheat boilers, designed for a working pressure of 525 psi and a temperature of 850°F.

One of the great innovations in the *Himalaya* was the distilling machinery which distilled seawater continuously for both boiler-feed and domestic purposes and reduced the amount of fresh water that had to be carried. The space thus saved was utilized to augment the vessel's cargo carrying capacity, which in those days was an important consideration in passenger liners. The *Himalaya* could carry 200,000 cubic feet of general cargo and 235,000 cubic feet of refrigerated cargo in six holds and 'tween decks space.

Although the *Chusan* was somewhat smaller than the *Himalaya*, having been built for the P&O Company's Far Eastern service, she was just as impressive and although many of her features were similar to those in the larger vessel, to do justice to this pleasing and elegant ship it is only right that her accommodation is described in detail.

Once again the clean lines of the upperworks were enhanced by the complete absence of ventilating cowls, with all the necessary air-intakes being incorporated in the deckhouse sides. Again this provided a large unencumbered area of the Boat Deck for the first class passengers' leisure and recreation. As in the *Himalaya* there was plenty of protection from unpleasant winds behind glazed screens which continued the line of the forward deckhouse for some 60 feet aft. Most of the first class public rooms were on the Promenade Deck, laid out within a large deckhouse, while the after end of the deck was for the use of tourist class passengers, as a games area.

The 475 first class passengers could relax in public rooms decorated and furnished by Waring & Gillow Ltd and Maple Ltd of London, and H. H. Martyn & Co Ltd of Cheltenham. The main lounge on the Promenade Deck was the principal public room, with an attractive feature at either side of wide casement windows. Other outstanding points were the central panels which adorned the forward and after bulkheads, a number of which carried modelled and painted motifs that depicted incidents in the life of Kublai Khan, as related in the tales of Marco Polo. Forward of the lounge was a spacious library and writing room, the plan of which was determined by the curved sweep of the forward bulkhead, where there was a large painting depicting an Italian-style arcaded colonnade. The carpet, curtains and upholstery fabrics were in shades of blue and blue-grey, and side doors gave access to the Promenade Deck and the lounge.

Aft of the lounge was the dancing space where there was a central raised deckhead with multi-coloured concealed lighting. The platform for the band was arranged at the forward end and the sides of the room, like those in the *Himalaya*, took the form of folding and sliding glazed screens. Double doors and short corridors at the after end of the dancing space gave access to the Verandah Café, which was an informal room overlooking the swimming-pool. The after

The *Chusan's* first class sports deck was, like the *Himalaya's*, a large unencumbered area on the Boat Deck, with glazed screens to protect passengers from the wind.

(Author's collection)

The *Chusan's* spacious first class Library and Writing Room at the forward end of the Promenade Deck.   *(Author's collection)*

Chusan's principal first class public room was the main lounge on the Promenade Deck, with wide casement windows and decorative panels, one of which can be seen in this view.   *(Author's collection)*

The first class dance space in the *Chusan* with its folding and sliding glazed side screens. This view looks forward towards the main lounge.
      (Author's collection)

The *Chusan's* first class Verandah Café was an informal room overlooking the swimming-pool. *(Author's collection)*

The *Chusan's* first class dining saloon on D Deck was amidships and it seated 274 passengers.

(Author's collection)

The tourist class lounge in the *Chusan* was on A Deck, just forward of the sports area. This view is looking forward on the port side.

(Author's collection)

The *Chusan's* tourist class dining saloon on D Deck could seat 274 passengers, and this view looks aft on the port side.

(Author's collection)

end of the café was formed by folding glazed screens which, when opened, gave passengers unobstructed views of the pool. The dominant colour scheme was grey and ivory, with the hide-covered furniture in terracotta and grey, colours which were also used in the curtains.

Most of the first class cabins and staterooms were situated on A, B, C and D Decks and they were either single- or two-berth rooms. Amidships on B Deck, there were two de luxe suites and two de luxe cabins, all of which were air-conditioned. The de luxe suites also had private verandahs. Generally the furniture in the first class cabins was in mahogany, although in some A Deck rooms white sycamore was used.

The fully air-conditioned dining saloon was amidships on D Deck with access from the main entrance foyer. The compartment occupied the full breadth of the ship and could seat 274 passengers at tables for two, four and six. It was extended at the port side aft to form a private dining-room, or a children's dining-room. The wood panelling throughout was finished in Australian walnut, with contrasting Burry ash. Extensive use was made of mirror glass, especially at the forward end.

The 551 tourist class passengers were accommodated aft on six decks, from the Promenade Deck down to E Deck with the after end of the Promenade Deck being set aside for games and recreation. The swimming-pool was at the after end of A Deck, and forward of this was the lounge. This room was attractively decorated with painted panelling in soft pale-green and a white sycamore trim. Coral-coloured tapestry was chosen for the settees and easy chairs, and other furniture included occasional tables and card-tables in mahogany and sycamore. The Smoking Room was directly beneath the swimming-pool, on B Deck, and here the panelling was made up of betula and straight-grained ash,

with a central section at the forward end in tan-coloured hide. The tourist class promenade space was also situated on B Deck. Forward of the Smoking Room was the dancing space which covered the full width of the ship and had glazed, folding screens at either side. The tourist class children's playroom was on C Deck and the dining saloon, which had seating for 274 passengers, was on D Deck. It was panelled in mottled ash with feature panels of olive ash burr and contrasting pastel blue hide-covered panels arranged at the forward and after ends of the room. The dining chairs, which had open backs, were upholstered in blue hide to match the wall panels.

The tourist class cabins were situated on B, C, D and E Decks and they were two- or four-berth rooms which were all comfortably furnished. The accommodation for the 572 crew members was arranged on a similar basis to that on board the *Himalaya*, with ample mess and recreation rooms being provided.

Like the *Himalaya* the *Chusan* was a twin-screw vessel, each of which was driven by a set of geared turbines which developed 34,000 SHP and steam was supplied at 525psi and 850°F by four controlled superheat, Foster Wheeler boilers. Four turbo-generators supplied electrical power for heating and lighting and there were two emergency diesel generators. A distillation plant was fitted and this provided water for the boilers and for domestic use. The *Chusan* also had a capacity for 408,000 cubic feet of general cargo and 22,500 cubic feet of refrigerated cargo. She was equipped with 20 three-ton and two ten-ton derricks, with power for operating the derricks derived from 22 three-ton electric winches.

When the two new ships entered service they completely eclipsed all other vessels on the routes east of Suez and they were set to become two of the best loved liners of the post-war world.

The *Himalaya* alongside Southampton's Western Docks on 3 April 1971. Five days after this photograph was taken she sailed on a 23-day cruise to the Caribbean. *(Don Smith)*

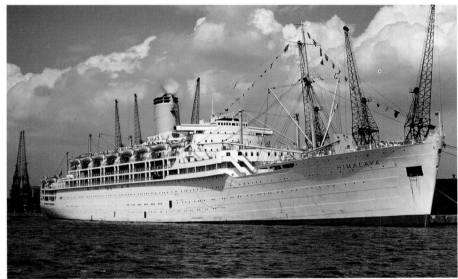

Himalaya alongside at Southampton during May 1973. *(Don Smith)*

On 18 May 1973 the *Himalaya* left Southampton for Cape Town and Sydney. Here she is shown steaming down Southampton Water at the start of the voyage. *(Don Smith)*

11 September 1949, and the *Himalaya* is berthed in Tilbury Docks for the first time. She is at 32 berth and directly astern of the new Orient liner *Orcades*.

(University of Cambridge - Vickers PLC)

Chapter Three

The Post-War World

On Wednesday 7 September 1949, just six days after being handed over to the P&O Company, Captain Stuart took his proud new ship to sea for a two-day cruise in the Channel. This was not, however, a commercial voyage as her 400 first class passengers were all company guests and the short journey was a test of the hotel services on board. The *Himalaya* returned to Southampton on Friday 9 September and the following morning she left the port bound for Tilbury where preparations would begin for her maiden voyage to Australia. During the afternoon of Sunday 11 September 1949 the great new liner wound her way slowly through the Thames Estuary and docked alongside No 32 berth in Tilbury Docks, directly astern of the new Orient liner *Orcades*, which had entered service in November 1948 and which had completed three round voyages between London and Sydney. There is no doubt that the two new liners looked resplendent in their gleaming livery, one corn-coloured and one white, as they both lay at Tilbury Docks together - each ship representing a capital outlay of over £3 million. That same evening, after dark, both vessels were floodlit, and the large lettering which spelt out their names, the *Himalaya's* in a reddish-brown paint and the *Orcades'* in green, was visible beneath their funnels from the opposite side of the river.

The *Orcades* left London on 20 September and 16 days later, at 4pm on Thursday 6 October 1949, the *Himalaya* sailed from Tilbury Landing Stage on her maiden voyage via Suez to India and Australia. Prior to her departure she had embarked a full complement of passengers in both classes and amongst these were Sir William Currie and Lady Currie, who was the vessel's sponsor at the launching exactly a year and a day before the start of her first commercial voyage. Captain D. M. Stuart, the Commodore of the P&O Fleet, was undertaking his final voyage before his well earned retirement. It is said that he had been appointed by the directors to command the ship during the maiden voyage partly as a gesture of appreciation of his distinguished service with the company. Captain H. C. C. Forsyth was appointed as the Staff Captain, and he would replace Captain Stuart on the latter's retirement.

Exactly seven days after leaving Tilbury the *Himalaya* arrived at Port Said and on the following day she left Port Suez following her first southbound transit of the Suez Canal. On Sunday 16 October she arrived off the Barren Rocks of Aden and she left the moorings at Steamer Point in the early hours of the following morning. She made a 24-hour call at Bombay on Thursday 20 October and spent most of Sunday 23 October moored in Colombo's busy harbour. The *Himalaya's* biggest and most enthusiastic welcoming crowds were at the Australian ports, first in Fremantle on 30 October and then Melbourne on 3 November, having passed the homeward-bound *Orcades* on the previous day. The *Himalaya* finally arrived in Sydney Harbour on Monday 7 November 1949 to

The *Himalaya's* floodlit funnel, showing her name in large lettering.
(Museum of London - Museum in Docklands Project)

The *Himalaya* loads cargo in preparation for her maiden voyage. *(University of Cambridge - Vickers PLC)*

a great welcome, and during her eleven-day stop-over in the port she was the centre of attraction at Circular Quay.

On Friday 18 November the *Himalaya* left Sydney and retraced her route to London, where she arrived alongside Tilbury's Landing Stage early on the morning of Thursday 22 December 1949, just in time for Christmas. Once again she had been fully booked and, having passed without any incidents, the maiden voyage was judged an unqualified success. On its completion Captain D. (Duggie) M. Stuart DSO retired from the sea after nearly 44 years and Captain H. C. C. Forsyth took command as arranged.

The *Himalaya's* first Christmas and New Year in service were spent alongside in Tilbury Docks and it was on Thursday 12 January 1950, a cold, bleak, winter's day that she left London for her second voyage east to Australia, once again sailing via Suez. Soon there came a sign of returning normality in post-war Britain when the P&O directors were able to announce that, during the summer of 1950, the *Himalaya* would be released from the Australian route for a short cruising season from Southampton, in tandem with the

brand new *Chusan*.

In February 1950 it was announced that the *Chusan* would commence her service with the company with a series of three cruises beginning in mid-July that year, and the demand for berths in both ships was so great that they were soon fully booked well in advance. The *Chusan* was the first to start her cruises, having been handed over to the company on 14 June. It had been thought that she might make her début with a charter to Cunard for four round voyages between Southampton and New York, to augment that company's transatlantic services, but in the event it appeared that she would not be ready on time and the *Stratheden* fulfilled the charter instead. However, the ship had been completed ahead of schedule and she was able to make a short two-day cruise to Rotterdam with members of P&O's shore staff and their families as passengers. During her stay in the Dutch port the Rotterdam Harbour authorities hospitably exempted the liner from the payment of harbour dues and while her passengers were conducted on a tour of the city during the Saturday, delegates to an international shipping conference, together

Captain D. M. Stuart DSO, flanked by Sir William and Lady Currie, together with the *Himalaya's* officers during the maiden voyage.   *(P&O)*

The *Himalaya* arrives at Sydney's Overseas Passenger Terminal on Monday 7 November 1949.   *(P&O)*

A lone yachtsman watches as the *Chusan* arrives in the Solent during her summer cruise programme in June 1950.   *(Museum of London - Museum in Docklands Project)*

The tug *Napia* manoeuvres the *Chusan* on the River Thames in September 1950, prior to her maiden voyage to the Far East.

(National Maritime Museum London)

Captain R. E. Tunbridge and his officers during the *Chusan's* maiden voyage to the Far East.

(P&O)

with civic dignitaries, were entertained to lunch on board. This short cruise ended on Sunday 18 June at Southampton and, despite the fact that there were still a number of workmen on board putting the finishing touches to the fitting out, it was a great success. In fact, the ship had been completed two weeks ahead of schedule and the company had been able to include an extra eight-day cruise from Southampton to Lisbon and Madeira; with fares starting at £25 it was sold out within two days of being announced.

The *Himalaya* left Southampton on Saturday 1 July, arriving in Lisbon two days later and in Madeira on 5 July, before returning to Southampton early on the morning of 9 July. Six days later, on Saturday 15 July 1950, the *Chusan* left Southampton on the first of her three scheduled cruises which was also to Lisbon and Funchal as well as Casablanca. The other two cruises took her into the Mediterranean for the first time with calls at Algiers, Malta and Naples, before returning to London on Sunday 27 August 1950. With fares starting at £36 these cruises represented excellent value and it is hardly surprising that there were over 12,000 applicants for only 5,000 berths.

Meanwhile the *Himalaya* had carried out two 14-day cruises to the Mediterranean and Casablanca which were also fully booked. It was quite clear that, in post-war Britain, cruising was going to be a very popular leisure activity. Following the end of their cruise programme both vessels returned to London and for ten days, until *Himalaya* left for Sydney, they were in their home port together. The *Chusan* left London on Friday 15 September 1950 for her first commercial passenger/cargo voyage which took her to Bombay via Suez where she arrived on the last day of the month. Such additional sailings to Bombay in the early autumn were customary before the Second World War and, of course, P&O liners were purpose-built for the route - the most famous being the fast liner *Viceroy of India*, which had been lost during the war. On 7 November 1950 *Chusan* left London for Hong Kong to augment the service which was being maintained by the smaller liners, *Carthage*, *Corfu* and *Canton*. In pre-war days P&O's Far Eastern service had extended to Japanese ports, but it would be some years before they would again feature on the P&O itinerary.

Captain Herb Bolles from New South Wales, who was serving in the BI Line's *Purnea* at the time, remembers passing the *Chusan* when the P&O chairman, Sir William Currie, was on board: 'All hands were on deck, eager to see this fine post-war P&O passenger ship. When we were close enough to read each other's name clearly, our jovial Chief Officer said, "Call her up Third, and ask what ship?" Not to be outdone, the reply came back like lightning: "*Chusan* ...and who are you?"' However, on board the *Chusan* it wasn't all plain sailing and Richard (Dickie) Firth remembers that during those early days there were considerable problems with funnel smuts on the after decks: 'One passenger put in a claim that her fur coat had been singed when she had left it on a deck chair by the pool whilst she was at lunch. I also remember one occasion during my evening 8-12 watch when the Chief Officer came to me in a "real tizzy". He wanted to know why I hadn't altered course when the boiler-room had blown soot. Fortunately we had a Sperry Course Recorder and I was able

to show him that I had, and once satisfied he took me to the Boat Deck where there was an enormous heap of smouldering soot. Thankfully no passengers had been in the vicinity at the time.' This was a problem which the company would soon have to address.

John Crawford, the *Chusan's* Purser, recalls her first voyage to the Far East. They enjoyed good weather throughout the voyage and, 'The *Chusan* arrived on time at Lymeun Pass where we picked up the pilot and then slowly steamed through the myriad of hooting craft in the harbour to our berth at Kowloon, where we received a tumultuous reception from the crowds on the jetty.'

At 9pm on Sunday 4 February 1951, in the Arabian Sea, the newest pair of P&O liners passed each other at sea for the first time. The *Chusan*, which had left Aden the day before, was bound for Bombay and the *Himalaya* was westbound, steaming for Aden, Suez and home. A. P Herbert, who was a passenger in the *Himalaya*, captured the atmosphere on board the two ships in this poem which he wrote and presented to Captain Forsyth.

> *Ah, yes, the distant stranger in the night*
> *May leave no memory but one red light.*
> *But you should see two sisters pass in style,*
> *No further than a fraction of a mile,*
> *The latest, swiftest of a splendid Line,*
> *As like as bottles of noble wine.*
> *The house-flag flutters in a flood of light,*
> *Salute of sirens shocking the velvet night.*
> *Here are no strangers. Officers and man*
> *Are life-long members of a loyal clan.*
> *We crowd the rails, mere passengers, and yell,*
> *Tonight proud owners of the Line as well.*
> *Such vessels, for a century and more,*
> *Have made the sea as solid as the shore.*
> *Such ships have made all Capricorn a friend,*
> *And Sydney not much farther than Southend*
> *(And, may we whisper, every vessel flies*
> *The ancient flag of Private Enterprise).*
> *The lights, the signals, die. The sisters part*
> *But something bright long lingers in the heart:*
> *And British breasts may be allowed to swell,*
> *For here's a thing we still do rather well.*

There is no doubt that the poem expresses the feeling of the occasion, but the *Chusan* was heading for some unwelcome publicity when she arrived in Bombay two days later. Of her 1,045 passengers, some 350 had contracted influenza, and the Indian authorities ordered them into quarantine. As the arrangements ashore were clearly inadequate for such numbers, it was first thought that they would have to remain on board and the ship would be delayed in the port for five days. However, a solution to the problem was found in the shape of two BI ships which were lying light in the port and to which the affected passengers could be transferred. *Chusan* was able to continue her voyage having been delayed for only a few hours and she arrived in Hong Kong without further incident on 20 February 1951.

Despite this minor problem, the two new P&O liners had been a resounding success during their first 18 months of service.

The *Chusan* in dock at Tilbury.

(Museum of London - Museum in Docklands Project)

Chapter Four

A New Profile

When the *Himalaya* left London on 5 September 1951, she had a full passenger list for what was just another routine voyage to Australia. On her way east she called at Ceuta in North Africa and then at the usual ports *en route* to Fremantle where she arrived on 29 September. However, during the journey it became clear that there were serious problems with the port engine, and when she arrived at Melbourne on 3 October an examination revealed that much of the blading from the HP and IP turbines had been stripped. After steaming to Sydney on one engine the turbines were examined more closely and it was decided that she would have to steam to the UK on only one engine. She left Sydney on 15 October and twelve days out, at 5.20am on 27 October 1951, when the ship was in the Indian Ocean between Fremantle and Colombo, a 21-year-old passenger, Miss E. C. Bandt, of Geelong, Victoria, was reported missing and a search of the ship was started. It was established that she had been seen last at 1.15am that morning sitting on the ship's rail. The ship was then turned round to retrace her course and after searching for the best part of the day, Miss Brandt was officially listed as 'Presumed lost at sea between 17° - 44'S/101° - 26'E and 16° - 31'S/100° - 20'E' and the liner resumed her course for Colombo. The *Himalaya* finally arrived in Southampton on 18 November, where the repairs were to be carried out. Whilst she was lying alongside the city's 107 berth, the Royal Mail steamer *Asturias*, which was being moved from 108 berth to the Eastern Docks, collided with her. Fortunately damage to the *Himalaya* was superficial and in the following week she was moved into No 6 dry dock in the Eastern Docks. However, her troubles were still not over for, on Monday 10 December, while she was leaving the dry dock following her engine repairs, a gust of wind caught the ship and carried her towards the quay where a crane was caught by the forward part of the *Himalaya's* superstructure and pushed along its rails, before it overturned and fell into the water at 49 berth. Fortunately, tugs regained control of the *Himalaya* and took her to a nearby berth, where repairs to her newly damaged superstructure platework and bent deck rails were carried out. Happily, the remainder of the overhaul passed off without incident and on 30 December 1951 the *Himalaya* left Southampton to undergo her main machinery trials in the Channel.

Himalaya's next Australian voyage started from Southampton on 3 January 1952, and Norman Morris, an Assistant Carpenter who had joined the ship during her

The *Himalaya* alongside Tilbury's 31 shed in the early 1950s.

(Museum of London - Museum in Docklands Project)

The *Chusan* outward bound from London in the early 1950s.

(Alex Duncan)

In June 1952 the *Chusan* had a 12ft-high funnel extension fitted, known as the 'Thorneycroft top'. This view shows her shortly afterwards.

(Ernest H. Cole)

The *Chusan* manoeuvres to her berth at Kowloon, Hong Kong.

(*P&O*)

In June 1953 the *Himalaya* was fitted with a 'Thorneycroft' funnel extension.
(Author's collection)

overhaul, remembers the final stages of the voyage from Fremantle: 'In those days, before air transport became available, it was a four-day voyage across the Great Australian Bight but, for many, it was preferable to making the long, hot and uncomfortable train journey. One of the passengers who embarked in Fremantle was an elderly lady who was well known in Australia as a medium and a spiritualist, and soon after she arrived on board she "held court" and announced that she had "foreseen" the *Himalaya* caught in a violent storm whilst crossing the Bight, and in her "vision" the vessel had foundered with great loss of life. Having caused a great deal of consternation on board she then promptly left the ship before we sailed. Some people, including a few crew members, had been rather unnerved by her prophecy and

they too disembarked. Their numbers included six stewards who claimed to have been influenced by her but, as severe weather had already been forecast on the radio, her prophecy was not particularly inspired and the captain was not at all pleased, but we sailed from Fremantle on time. Once at sea we did encounter some very bad weather in the Bight, but we reached Adelaide safely, and only one hour late, to find our six errant stewards waiting on the quayside. However, much to their astonishment, the captain would not allow them back on board and they were paid off, their places being taken by Australian stewards.'

Not long afterwards the *Chusan* was involved in an incident, when on Thursday 10 April, as she was leaving London for a voyage to the Far East, she was in collision with

The *Himalaya* at Sydney in the mid-1950s.
(P&O)

The *Chusan* leaving Tilbury Landing Stage for the Far East.

(Ernest H. Cole)

the steamer *Tanar*. Fortunately damage to both ships was slight and the *Chusan* was able to continue her voyage after only a short delay. When she returned to London on 3 June 1952 she went alongside No 9 shed in King George V Dock as usual and then into the nearby dry dock. The age-old problem of oil smuts on the passenger decks was to be remedied, and the answer which P&O had come up with was to fit a 12ft-high funnel extension known as the 'Thorneycroft' top, named after the company John I. Thorneycroft, who had designed it. Tests had shown that there were two ways of overcoming the problem of funnel smuts, the first by extending the height of the funnel and the second by increasing the velocity of the gases up the funnel. Many people thought that the appearance of the ship was definitely not improved by the addition but the P&O management considered that the results justified the change. On 26 June that year the *Chusan* made a series of two-week cruises from Southampton to the Mediterranean and the Atlantic Islands and from London to the Firth of Forth and the Fjords, and during each voyage the effects of the new funnel top were studied at regular intervals, as well as when the wind direction changed and courses were altered. It was found that the funnel gases did not tend to curl downwards behind the funnel, and it was also noted that there was a definite improvement in cleanliness of both the decks and the paintwork.

The *Himalaya's* summer cruise programme in 1952 consisted of just two 21-day voyages into the Mediterranean, which took her to Malta, Rhodes, Trieste, Venice, Palma, Naples, Istanbul and Piraeus. It was during the first of these cruises, whilst the ship was berthed at Trieste on Tuesday 15 July, that a sudden storm blew up which lasted nearly half an hour. The *Himalaya*, which was alongside the quay, was pushed away from her berth by high winds and the passenger gangway fell onto the quay. Unfortunately, two passengers were just starting to climb the gangway when it fell, and they had to be taken to hospital with serious injuries. The resulting litigation, which lasted for over two years, resulted in the Court of Appeal ruling that, despite the exemption clauses printed in their tickets, passengers were entitled to sue shipowners for injuries caused in such circumstances. In fact this was a most unusual incident in which the oil tanker *British Fortune*, berthed nearby, was also pushed against the quay wall and damaged, which indicates the severity of the storm.

During 1952 came the announcement that, after an absence of eleven years, the P&O vessels on the Far Eastern run would resume calling at the Japanese ports of Yokohama and Kobe, for with the Japanese post-war 'economic miracle' well under way, the company could not afford to ignore the resulting trade. However, it was January 1954 before the *Chusan* made her first call at Yokohama, and before this the liner was involved in an unfortunate accident in the Straits of Dover, which disrupted her cruise programme for the summer of 1953. During the afternoon of Friday 12 June, the *Chusan* left Tilbury Landing Stage for a 21-day cruise into the Mediterranean. It was her first cruise of the season, having just arrived back in London from the Far East on 26 May, and soon after leaving the Thames she ran into thick fog and speed was reduced. She steamed through The Downs without incident but, at 8.51pm that evening, when she was about a mile off the South Goodwin light vessel, and just under six miles from Dover's East Pier Head, she collided with the 6,165-ton Harrison Line cargo ship SS *Prospector*, which was bound for London from the West Indies. The smaller vessel sustained damage in a 'V' shape around the area of her chain locker and No 1 hold, starting 7ft abaft her stem and extending across the ship over a length of 30ft at deck level down through five strakes to 15ft below water level. No 1 hold, with its cargo of bagged sugar and barrels of spirits, was flooded and her 'tween deck area was awash. She was able to anchor, but she put out a call for assistance from tugs. The *Chusan* was also extensively damaged with a 25ft-long gash, one foot wide, on the prow, about 20ft above the water-line. Fortunately no one was injured on either ship and the *Chusan* also anchored in order that the damage could be assessed. Early next morning, when the fog had lifted, both ships were able to get under way. The *Prospector* put in to Dover, but the *Chusan* had to make her way back to Tilbury and she arrived off Gravesend at 1pm on Saturday 13 June, where she anchored. Soon after her arrival the P&O deputy chairman and other company officials, together with officials from Lloyd's and the Ministry of Transport, were embarked to survey the damage. After a rather tense three-hour wait, during which time rumours abounded, Captain Gerry Randall, the Staff Commander, was able to announce over the loudspeakers that the cruise would go on. However, the inevitable delays which would be incurred meant that the itinerary would have to be altered and a proposed call at Genoa was cancelled. That evening, at 7pm, the liner was made fast alongside the Tilbury Landing Stage and work began to repair the damage. For the 900 passengers it was almost 'business as usual' with all the entertainment going on as usual, and with the bonus that they were able to go ashore to see friends and relatives who were in the area. During the night, with floodlights illuminating her bows, work to repair the damaged hull continued without a break and by the late afternoon of Sunday 14 June a large metal plate had been welded on and painted white. Although it was just a temporary repair, it was only visible at close quarters and when the *Chusan* finally left Tilbury, 55 hours behind schedule, there was little sign of the damage. After calling at Messina, Istanbul, Piraeus and Casablanca, the liner returned to Southampton on 3 July 1953 and the following day she left for a 14-day cruise which, once again, took her into the Mediterranean. This voyage concluded on 18 July at Tilbury Landing Stage and three days later she entered the dry dock at Tilbury for permanent repairs to be made to her bow. When the *Chusan* left London on 24 July, bound for Leith where she embarked passengers for a Baltic cruise, the collision with the *Prospector* was just a distant memory.

Meanwhile, in May 1953 at Tilbury, there was another change of command on board the *Himalaya* when Captain D. G. H. O. Baillie took over from Captain S. W. S. Dickson. These are Captain Baillie's first memories of the great ship: 'The first thing to strike me about the *Himalaya* was her size. Compared to my recent commands, she seemed immense. It took me literally weeks to get used to her height above the water-line, and to her length from stem to stern. There was one particular spot in my day-cabin from which you could see

both the Red Ensign at her stern and the company's flag flying from her jack-staff; and the stretch of deck between them was awe-inspiring until you had become accustomed to it.

My next strong impression was the *Himalaya's* undoubted atmosphere - a quality produced more tangibly to the cubic foot in a ship than in any other object constructed by the hands of man. The *Himalaya* was always very special. Being the first P&O mail-ship to be built after the war and therefore a symbol to us all of returning luxury and normality after the abnormality of the war years, there had always been lavished on her a very great deal of care, attention and affection. She had been happily commanded in turn by Captain D. M. Stuart, Captain H. C. C. Forsyth and Captain S. W. S. Dickson; and Hugh Forsyth, who had also been her first Staff Commander, Gavin Maclean, her first Chief Officer, and Douglas Pullinger, her first Purser, had poured their knowledge, experience, energy, resourcefulness, in fact their own personalities, into the common pool in order to make this wonderful new ship a success.

By the time I took over command of the *Himalaya* she had to her credit three strenuous cruising seasons interspersed with regular voyages to Australia during the winter months; and already she had developed a tradition of something more than excellence. On 29 May, as the feverish mood of those days immediately before the Coronation was rising to unpredictable heights of enthusiasm, we cast off from the Tilbury Landing Stage and slipped down the London River on our first cruise of the 1953 season. I discovered at once that my new ship had not only looks but performance. She was fast - I knew that already. 21 knots was her comfortable speed, and at 23 she glided through the seething water with curiously little fuss and an exhilarating feeling of being "on her toes". And she handled superbly.

The first cruise was a strenuous test of the organization for which the *Himalaya* was justly famous. Into that fortnight we packed not only our own Coronation celebrations, but a festivity of some kind at every port. On 2 June we were in the Mediterranean steaming at speed in fine, warm weather. There were cocktail-parties, a Gala Dinner and a Coronation Ball; the Queen's health was drunk "on the house", and every passenger received a handsome memento, and every member of the ship's company a souvenir medallion.

Next day we arrived at Naples; and here the *Himalaya* had been lent by the company to the British members of NATO, who acted as hosts to their colleagues at a reception held on board. The whole ship and her entire staff were placed at their service. The *Himalaya* looked magnificent, her great yellow funnel floodlit, her decks and public rooms blazing with light and bright with decorations.'

The cruise described by Captain Baillie finished at Southampton on 12 June and after completing two more cruises, the *Himalaya* returned to Southampton where she spent five days in dry dock, during which time she too was fitted with a 'Thorneycroft' funnel top. Following this she resumed her summer cruising schedule and, once again, the story is taken up by Captain Baillie whose description of *Himalaya's* cruises of the early 1950s still holds good today: 'I certainly enjoyed the cruising season enormously for its infinite variety and a general atmosphere of light-heartedness.

The *Himalaya* moored in Colombo Harbour in late 1953.
(Norman Pound)

There is something about a shipful of people all intent on leaving their cares over the stern that is most invigorating. The master of a cruise liner has only one real bugbear, and that is, fog. Cruises are planned on a tight schedule, and in the 30 hours between the end of one cruise and the beginning of the next, the ship has to be entirely re-stored and cleaned. The *Himalaya* would dock at Southampton between eight or nine o'clock on a Friday morning to disembark her 1,100 passengers, and by the Saturday forenoon she would be spick and span once more, decks scrubbed, alleyways and public rooms gleaming, and spotless cabins ready for their next occupants, every piece of linen changed, and fresh flowers everywhere. The amount of hard work and detailed organization involved was phenomenal, but on each occasion it was achieved with perfect smoothness. But fog could disrupt the entire programme, complicating berthing arrangements and boat-train schedules as well as cutting short our brief stay in port. But cruising is also great fun. The average mail-ship passenger travelling on business, or back from leave, may take life with a certain degree of gravity. Cruise passengers belong to a totally different category. Most of them have been saving up for this fortnight and looking forward to it for the best part of a year. They are going to enjoy every minute of it, extract every ounce of excitement out of it, and make the utmost of every ray of Mediterranean sunshine. They endure torments of blistering sunburn in order to acquire the obligatory tan; and if the sun fails to shine - which it not infrequently does in direct defiance of the travel posters - their dismay and disappointment can be pitiable. They expect organized entertainment throughout their waking hours and never seem to tire of the incessant round of tombolas, race meetings, treasure hunts, cinema shows, dances and deck sports planned for their amusement while the ship is at sea. Going ashore is the prime objective, although their criterion of a place is often a matter of its shopping facilities rather than its interest or fame; and there is no doubt that the ideal cruise from the passengers' point of view would consist of a port at least every other day, and not too long a stretch of open sea in between.

Many of our passengers had cruised in the *Himalaya* every season since her first commissioning; some had fallen in love with the ship while travelling on the Australian run; others were experiencing their first sea voyage, and their reactions were often refreshing. There were many personal highlights: my first visit to the Acropolis; the startling sophistication of the new hotels at Casablanca; a luncheon, given on the occasion of our first call at Cannes; an open-air performance of 'Carmen' in moonlight at Naples; and at Madeira, the apparent survival of a curiously feudal society, as though two wars had passed that lovely island by and left it utterly unchanged.'

On 19 December 1954 the *Chusan* left London for a voyage east and her first visit to Japan, calling at Yokohama and then her final destination of Kobe on 25 April 1955. However, on 5 January 1955, whilst she was moored in the very busy port of Colombo, a sudden squall blew up and the liner broke free from her moorings. As she swung round with the tide she collided with the 7,591-ton Ellerman Line steamer *City of Cardiff*, which was also at moorings nearby. Fortunately there were no injuries and there was only superficial damage to both ships, and the *Chusan* was able to sail from the port bound for Penang, Singapore, Hong Kong, Yokohama and Kobe. She arrived at Yokohama at 10am on 22 January, to an enthusiastic welcome. The *Chusan* was the largest liner to call at any Japanese port since the end of the war and a very busy programme of events had been organized by the civic authorities and by Captain Bodley. The ship herself was certainly looking her best, having been given a new coat of paint during her two-day stop-over in Hong Kong.

On 31 May 1954, when returning from her second voyage to Japan, the *Chusan* was in collision with the MV *Sydney Star* in the River Thames. The damage was confined to one section of teak taffrail on B Deck and rails on A Deck, and it was soon repaired in time for her summer cruising season which started on 12 June that year, and which took her into the Mediterranean, and to the Atlantic Isles. The five cruises were completed at Southampton on 21 September and the following day she arrived back in London. However, owing to a national dock strike, it was decided to send the *Chusan* to Rotterdam for her annual overhaul and she spent eight days in the Dutch port where the necessary work was carried out, including permanent repairs to the ship's guard-rails. By 6 October the *Chusan* was back in London and three days later she sailed for Hong Kong.

The *Himalaya* also experienced her share of 'firsts' in the early 1950s, including one notable event, the first cruise from Australia by a P&O ship since August 1939, which she undertook at the end of 1954. She arrived in Sydney on 22 December 1954 and two days later, on Christmas Eve, she left the port on a nine-day cruise with over 1,100 passengers embarked. The voyage across the Tasman Sea took the *Himalaya* to Auckland and Wellington. It was Captain Baillie's last round voyage to Australia before his retirement and his memories of the cruise show what an unqualified success it was: 'We left Sydney on Christmas Eve in splendid weather, a full ship. Some of us had been slightly apprehensive lest the passenger list should contain a rowdy element, not unlikely at the peak of the holiday season; but our complement of passengers turned out to be one of the most pleasant and best behaved that I had ever carried.

Rounding the north-east corner of North Island we found ourselves on a night of brilliant moonlight steaming down the Hauraki Gulf, at the foot of which lay Auckland, our first port of call. Here I was properly thankful to the Providence that watches over the shipmaster venturing for the first time into unfamiliar waters, for as we passed between the islands with which the Gulf is strewn, such as Poor Knight's Island and the Hen & Chickens, a curious phenomenon appeared. The radar screen kept showing up innumerable islands where none existed on the calm waters of the Gulf, which stretched ahead of us as clear as daylight beneath the summer moon. There is, I believe, a scientific explanation for this odd discrepancy between the scene in reality and that recorded on the radar screen; nevertheless it is an eerie experience. In any case, I remained on the bridge all that night as we were in sight of land, and next day we entered Auckland Harbour.

Leaving again at midnight, we were in Hawke Bay by the following afternoon, and I took the ship well inshore to have a look at Napier. The people of Napier, having been advised of our coming, had turned out in their hundreds to have a look at us, for I imagine that in this part of the world there are not many opportunities of seeing such a ship as the *Himalaya*; and indeed, as she steamed into view, white and gold in the hot sunshine, and leaving a foaming wake in the dark blue water, she must have been a sight worth coming many miles to see.

For the greater part of the night I kept on the bridge, navigating round the coast, bringing the ship next morning into the magnificent land-locked harbour of Wellington.'

The cruise was a resounding success and *Himalaya* arrived back in Sydney on New Year's Day 1955. An extract from the minutes of the Voyage Committee Meeting which took place after the *Himalaya* arrived back in London on 2 February 1955, read as follows: 'The Chairman congratulated the Commodore on the most successful Australian cruise and mentioned especially the excellent publicity obtained as a result of the *Himalaya* entering Napier Bay.'

Not only had the two ships gained a new profile, but they had earned a reputation for excellence the world over.

During the Suez Crisis of 1956 both the *Himalaya* and the *Chusan* were routed via the Cape of Good Hope. Here the *Himalaya* is shown at Cape Town, with Table Mountain in the background.

(*Alex Duncan*)

Chapter Five

The Orient & Pacific Line

The first five months of 1955 saw the *Chusan* plying her route between London and Japan, and in February that year, when she was on a homeward voyage between Singapore and Port Said, an Indian woman passenger was taken ill with suspected smallpox. Although she was landed and taken to hospital at Port Said and the remaining passengers were vaccinated, when the ship arrived in London on 2 March it was thought that they would have to be quarantined. However, it was decided that they should be allowed to land on condition that all their names and addresses were kept by the company and the Ministry of Health. It had been a very busy voyage for the ship's medical staff for not only did they have the smallpox problem to handle, but an 18-month-old boy had a mild attack of poliomyelitis during the journey. Fortunately, by the time the liner had docked in London he had recovered and he was not sent to hospital.

During the summer months the two ships carried out their cruise programmes, the *Chusan* from Southampton and the *Himalaya* from Sydney. The *Himalaya*, in fact, made the first post-war cruise by a P&O liner to Suva, Noumea and Port Moresby. The ship was fully booked for the voyage and at Suva the band of the Fijian Defence Force turned out to welcome the ship, as did many of the residents. At Noumea, the next port of call, a Ball was held at the Town Hall in honour of the visit, and at Port Moresby, which revived vivid memories of the Second World War for many Australians, there were a number of organized visits to the war cemetery at Bomana. Indeed, many passengers had booked berths on the cruise in order to visit the cemetery. The voyage home to Sydney through the Great Barrier Reef made a fitting climax to a very successful 'first' for the *Himalaya*.

The *Chusan's* summer cruise programme brought her some less welcome publicity when, on the final cruise which had started at Southampton on 27 August 1955, an anonymous message was received at Scotland Yard to the effect that a bomb had been placed on board. The ship was in Naples at the time and security on board was tightened, with thorough searches being carried out. When the ship sailed during the evening of 1 September, the Italian authorities kept in close touch with the liner and further searches were carried out when she called at Messina the following day. Fortunately the whole incident proved to be a hoax, but it was reassuring for the passengers to know that such incidents were taken very seriously and dealt with efficiently. After calling at Piraeus, Beirut, Rhodes, Barcelona and Vigo the *Chusan* returned to Southampton on 17 September, and on the last day of that month she left London bound once again for the Far East.

The *Himalaya's* final cruise of 1955 was a Christmas Cruise from Sydney to New Zealand, during which she carried 1,160 passengers to Auckland and Wellington. Despite rough weather off the coast of New Zealand, which caused the cancellation of an intended diversion to Hawke Bay, the cruise was a resounding success and soon after her return to Sydney the *Himalaya* left for London.

When she sailed on her next voyage to Australia on 17 February 1956, among the passengers for Colombo was Lady Churchill, being seen off by Sir Winston Churchill who had retired as Prime Minister in the previous year. Both of them were welcomed on board by P&O's deputy chairman, Sir Donald Anderson, who also hosted a special luncheon party. Afterwards Sir Winston toured the ship before disembarking shortly before she sailed. On her return to London from Sydney in April 1956 to take up her summer cruise programme, the *Himalaya* brought over the Australian cricket team for the test series.

The summer of 1956 was dominated by news from the Middle East. In March that year, as a result of an agreement reached in October 1954, the main body of British troops left the Suez Canal Zone and on 13 June 1956, three days before the date which had been agreed, the last British troops left Egypt when the rearguard handed over Navy House to the Governor of Port Said, and then left by sea. Political events moved quickly after that and on 20 July 1956 Britain and America withdrew their offer of financial aid to Egypt to assist with the building of the Aswan Dam. For President Nasser of Egypt this left only one other source of revenue - the Suez Canal, and on 26 July 1956 he announced its immediate nationalization. The next day in London, the Prime Minister, Sir Anthony Eden, instructed the Chiefs of Staff to prepare plans for the reoccupation of the Suez Canal Zone, just over six weeks after the last British troops had left Egypt. Unfortunately from the very start political thinking was confused. Was the idea to topple Nasser or was it to 'internationalize' the Suez Canal? What were the long-term aims of a military occupation and how would the problem of terrorism which had dogged the Suez Canal base prior to the withdrawal be overcome? That summer, as seemingly endless negotiations dragged on, these were just some of the questions which divided public opinion in Britain.

For the *Himalaya* August 1956 brought her final cruise of the summer season and at 3.11pm on 27 August she left Tilbury Landing Stage for what should have been a routine voyage to Australia. She was commanded by Captain H. P. Mallet, who had taken over two weeks earlier on 13 August, and her Chief Engineer was Mr F. H. Goodall. Three days after leaving Tilbury, at 6.45pm on Thursday 30 August 1956, when the *Himalaya* was in a position Lat 36° - 35'N/Long 00° - 08'E, off the coast of Algeria, there was an explosion by the domestic refrigeration room which was situated on the starboard side, in the working alleyway on E Deck. The resulting blast caused severe burns and injuries to a number of crew members and Mr A. K. McConnell, the First Refrigerating Engineer, was killed instantly. Altogether 14 men were injured and it was clear that three of those were in a critical condition having suffered terrible burns.

Mrs Penny MacLean, a Nursery Stewardess, recalls that evening: 'I can remember the evening of Thursday 30 August 1956 well. I had just come off nursery duty and I was in my cabin washing my hair when there was an urgent knocking on my door. I opened it to find a very ashen-faced Second Steward, Alan Waterman, standing there. He told me that

The *Chusan* in King George V Dock, London, with her funnel floodlit.
(Alex Duncan)

there had been a bad explosion and asked me to report immediately to the ship's hospital at the after end of B Deck. I was a children's nanny and I had no real experience of nursing, but I rushed along to see what I could do to help. When I arrived there it was an appalling scene as stretcher after stretcher, each carrying very badly burned men, was being brought in. I can remember that they quickly tannoyed the passengers for volunteers to help the injured, and I was assigned to an Indian doctor who had come forward. It was terrible to see and to hear the suffering of the badly burned men.'

Second Steward Alan Waterman, who had been in an office near the refrigerating compartment checking linen lists, had been told of a strange hissing noise from the refrigeration machinery and he had gone along the alleyway to report it to the refrigeration engineers. Both First Refrigeration Engineer McConnell and Second Refrigeration Engineer J. McLaverty went quickly to the machinery room and as Alan Waterman walked back to his office, 'I saw the First Refrigeration Engineer start to run and he got ahead of the Second. The explosion occurred as soon as he got to the compartment.'

As the refrigeration machinery compartment was situated close to the cabins occupied by the Goan stewards it was inevitable that they would bear the brunt of the blast and, in fact, nine of the casualties were from the ship's Goan catering staff. However, as the ship's main propulsion machinery was unaffected the *Himalaya* was still able to steam at full speed and, in Captain Mallet's own words: 'Additional medical supplies were requested by radio from the International Radio Medical Centre at Rome. Algiers agents were advised of the situation, and casualties, and it was decided to proceed to Algiers where we would have arrived at about 1.30am on 31 August. A message was received from Algiers that a curfew was enforced at the port from midnight and consequently after consultation with the Staff Commander, Chief Officer, Surgeon, Chief Engineer and Purser, it was decided to

proceed with all speed to Malta in the hope that medical supplies would be dropped by air on the way by the International Radio Medical Centre.'

All that night the *Himalaya* steamed hard for Malta and on the morning of Friday 31 August, despite the intensive care which they had been receiving, two of the injured Goans died from the second degree burns which they had received. That same morning, at a small ceremony, the body of the First Refrigeration Officer was committed to the deep in a position Lat 37° - 10'N/Long 05° - 02'E. He had taken the full force of the explosion which, it transpired, had been caused by a spark from an electrical switch which had ignited methyl chloride gas leaking from the refrigeration machinery. At 4.15am on Saturday 1 September the *Himalaya* berthed in Malta's Grand Harbour, where the injured were landed at St Angelo Jetty and taken by a relay of ambulances to Bighi Naval Hospital.

The *Himalaya* herself was able to slip her berth at 10pm that night to continue her voyage and 48 hours later she arrived at Port Said. Despite the fact that the Suez Canal Company had been nationalized, there was little out of the ordinary about the ship's southbound transit of the waterway, and at 6.45pm on Wednesday 5 September 1956 she left Port Suez for Aden and Bombay. However, back in Valletta on that same day, another of the Goans had died from the injuries he received in the explosion seven days earlier. The *Himalaya's* tragic voyage ended at Sydney on the morning of Friday 28 September 1956, and Captain Mallet learned that his route home was to be via Cape Town and Las Palmas.

Meanwhile, on 1 September 1956, the *Chusan* was about to leave Southampton for the final cruise of her UK summer season, a 14-day voyage to the Western Mediterranean. She returned to Southampton on 15 September, and then steamed round to London the following day. Three days later it was announced that her next voyage to Hong Kong, for which she would leave London on 27 September, was to be

The *Himalaya* leaving Singapore's Keppel Harbour in the late 1950s.   *(P. Cranch)*

routed via Cape Town. Unfortunately, this longer voyage meant that a surcharge of 20 per cent would be added to her fares, but there was little choice since political tensions had heightened as British and French preparations to invade Egypt neared completion, and with the Israeli Army about to invade Egypt through Sinai, the British government had warned shipping to keep clear of the Levant area and the Suez Canal. The *Chusan's* first voyage to Hong Kong via Las Palmas, Cape Town, Durban, Bombay, Colombo, Penang and Singapore took just over five weeks, and she made three such voyages between 27 September 1956 and 12 June 1957, when she started her UK summer cruising season.

John Crawford, the *Chusan's* Purser, remembers one amusing incident which happened during the ship's first cruise that year, a 14-day voyage to Tenerife, Casablanca and Barcelona: 'At each port shore excursions were handled by a local tour operator and at Casablanca this was done by two brothers named Laredo. They worked hard to promote the tourist trade and they also maintained a good liaison with the Moroccan royal family, and in June that year, when we were two days out of Casablanca, we received a cable from London stating that Prince Abdullah, the youngest son of the Sultan of Morocco, would inspect the ship and we were asked to lay on a reception for him and a number of local dignitaries, including the Governor of the city and a government minister. As the ship was fully booked it was decided to host a reception in the first class library and a suitable menu was arranged. On our arrival in Casablanca, and at the appointed time, a guard of honour of Lascars in full regalia was stationed at the bottom of the gangway. However, this was a family who kept the Queen and Prince Philip waiting for a considerable time when they visited the country, and the

Prince and his escort arrived at the gangway over an hour late, with no hint of an apology. Needless to say the Guard of Honour was beginning to wilt by that time, but they did their best. In those days it was the practice in all our ships to announce meal times by a Bell Boy who would walk through the public rooms sounding a gong. No sooner had the reception for Prince Abdullah and the VIPs got under way, than, to the utter astonishment of everyone present, through the port door came a Goan Bell Boy joyfully sounding the dinner gong, and he proceeded to wend his way right through the centre of the room where Captain Last was entertaining his distinguished guests. Still playing the gong he went out through the starboard door leaving the bemused Prince asking for the meaning of this strange English "ritual". However, the captain was not amused and he asked me to discipline the steward responsible. However, when I asked why he had continued through the library when obviously there was such an important function on, he replied, "Sir, I always go that way". How could one discipline him for doing his duty as best he could? Fortunately it did not detract from the success of the occasion, but I'm still not sure whether the Moroccan royal visitor understood what the "ritual" was all about.'

The next cruise in the *Chusan's* schedule took her into the Mediterranean where she visited Naples, and following that she made an eight-day cruise to Lisbon and Madeira. Two hours after leaving Funchal on 25 July, two stowaways were found hiding in waste bins, obviously hoping to make the three-day voyage to Southampton. However, the ship paid a very rare visit to the tiny Atlantic island of Porto Santo, just 34 miles north-east of Madeira, where they were handed over to the Portuguese authorities.

On 20 January 1958 P&O announced that it was to

introduce a transpacific service, which would create new routes and thus extend its Far Eastern and Australian voyages far beyond their traditional ports of call. The main factor which was in the minds of the P&O management was the lucrative trade in the Pacific area, and in particular along the West Coast of North America. The Orient Line, which was part of the P&O Group, were extending their voyages into the Pacific, and it was decided to combine the P&O and Orient Line fleets to provide three new routes around the Pacific Ocean. The first would take the traditional Australian voyages beyond Sydney to create a new service linking Australia, New Zealand and the West Coast of North America. The second would link Hong Kong and Japan with the US West Coast and the third route would be a triangular service between Australia, Asia and the USA. The new service was to be called the 'Orient & Pacific Line' and it was to be inaugurated by the *Himalaya* in March 1958.

The late 1950s were the heyday of the post-war liner voyages to the Far East and Australia, and Richard Greenwood of Swansea recalls the first leg of *Himalaya's* long inaugural voyage which left Tilbury on 15 February 1958 and arrived in Sydney on 18 March 1958: 'Having arrived on the quayside at Tilbury on a cold, damp morning in February and having dumped our baggage on the dockside, we slowly mounted the covered gangway to find our cabins in the *Himalaya*. This time our two young children had an adjoining cabin, a welcome innovation which provided more space for dressing and for stowing our belongings, as well as giving them a little play space.

Having edged her way out of the narrow locks of Tilbury Docks the *Himalaya* briefly anchored in mid-river before setting sail. For us it was time to organize the youngsters for their 5.30pm dinner before returning to our cabin to unpack the suitcases. Soon the closing bars of "The Roast Beef of Old England" summoned us to the dining saloon and the routine of the voyage had begun.

When we awoke next morning it was to dark skies and a "lumpy" Channel, but soon there was boat drill and the opening of the children's nurseries, where our youngest daughter, fearing she was going to be abandoned for the voyage, protested loudly. That morning, as I sat in the lounge, I was able to study the passenger list, and the remarkable cross-section of P&O's clientele became evident. There were "crusty" colonels *en route* to India, jaunty Australian Navy officers, priests and sisters, doctors, professors and actors, as well as many young families. Some of our more distinguished fellow passengers were the newly appointed Governor-General of Australia and his family, and the actress Jessie Matthews.

The Bay of Biscay was surprisingly calm for February and, as the weather got warmer, the Bosun optimistically supervised the filling of the small swimming-pool at the after end of A Deck. We settled down to a high calorie diet, faultlessly served by the silent Goan waiters who were all the more attentive as our host at table was the company's Superintendent Purser. He was *en route* to Colombo where he was to transfer to one of the *Straths* - serving as a superior sort of "bus inspector", switching from one ship to another to keep a weather eye on operations at sea.

On the third morning we passed the impressive Rock of Gibraltar and thereafter the weather deteriorated. Cold winds from the north whipped up the sea into a long swell from the port quarter and it steadily increased in intensity as far as Sicily when, at dinner on the fourth day, a rogue wave caught the ship. In the dining saloon it caused chaos as diners clutched the tables for safety and a good proportion of the crockery and food slid unceremoniously to the deck.

Port Said produced a welcome break and after passing the breakwater we approached our berth at 6am on the morning of Saturday 22 February, exactly a week after we had left London. The Moorish-style architecture of the Suez Canal Company's former offices and the flashing neon signs proclaiming the merits of 'Johnny Walker' whisky were sufficient to lure many passengers ashore to sample the dubious delights of the street vendors and the Simon Artz department store which opened its doors as soon as a big passenger ship arrived in Port Said - whatever the hour. By 7.30am we had returned to the ship laden down with leather cushions, dates, Turkish Delight and a small ivory camel. After negotiating the long, snake-like gangway of pontoon floats we were able to recover at breakfast in the *Himalaya's* saloon. That morning we watched the bum-boat men, addressing both passengers and crew with feigned obsequiousness and cunning as they attempted, good naturedly, to rook all who took an interest. Calling all their customers "McGregor" they sold anything from sandals to swordsticks. Another enduring memory is that of the "Gully-Gully" man, with his small, bewildered, squeaking yellow chicks. However, at noon the Canal convoy was joined and we steamed slowly south to Lake Timsah where the pilot was changed and a stream of northbound tankers passed us, bound for the Mediterranean. It was dusk before we weighed anchor and continued our slow passage south, with the Suez Canal searchlight pointing the way ahead.

The Red Sea was mild and quite pleasant and the officers had, by now, changed into their "whites". For the passengers the swimming-pool and its adjoining café had become the social focus, with the more energetic competing at quoits and deck tennis. With the calm seas and warmer weather the children's sports were held on the Games Deck, including an egg and spoon race and tug of war and culminating in the frantic crawling race for the under-twos.

We were quite thankful that it was late afternoon when the *Himalaya* steamed slowly towards the barren mountains that encircle Aden's harbour, for the weather was hot and humid. However, once we were secured to our buoys off Steamer Point we joined the queue of passengers waiting for the ship's launches which were running a shuttle service from the gangway to the pierhead at the centre of the dusty and undistinguished Crescent which formed the heart of Steamer Point. Here the beggars and hawkers were more persistent than those at Port Said. One of them had a goat which ate cigarettes and another offered taxi rides into the equally dusty and undistinguished town of Sheik Othman or to the Yemen border for two pounds. The shops were good for cameras, radios and binoculars at duty-free prices, but the hot, dusty and noisy streets had few attractions and a two-hour stay was more than sufficient.

The five-day voyage across the Arabian Sea passed pleasantly enough with mornings spent in the swimming-

The *Himalaya* is high and dry in Southampton's King George V Dry Dock. *(British Transport Dock Board)*

pool, slothful afternoons in the shade of the Promenade Deck and with the ship's orchestra to entertain us at afternoon tea. To while away the evenings and to aid digestion after five course dinners, there were films, concerts, dancing and guessing competitions (now called quizzes), although the formidable contest to find the "Brain of the Ship" was happily deferred until the weather cooled down.

The luxury of a full day's stop-over in Colombo on Sunday 2 March was much appreciated. The more adventurous among us chose a 72-mile car trip into the mountains to Kandy, with lunch at the Queen's Hotel for £2.17.6d (£2.88) a head. We opted for a shorter journey which was more suitable for children, and went to Victoria Park with its cinnamon gardens and temples with huge reclining Buddhas. We followed this with a swim in the surf in front of the Mount Lavinia Hotel, and a hot curry lunch with fresh pineapple. We were quite happy to spend the heat of the afternoon in the shade of the palm tees with gentle cooling breezes from the sea. An object of particular attention was my daughter's teddy bear which the Sinhalese called "wallaha", and in those days he was quite a novelty in Ceylon.

The voyage onward to Fremantle occupied six days and seven nights, and having said farewell to the travelling Purser, we were joined at our table by a genial tea-planter who had chosen a refreshing holiday at sea. He would stay with the *Himalaya* for her Pacific circuit from Sydney to Auckland, Suva, Honolulu, Vancouver and San Francisco and return the same way to Sydney and Colombo - a delightful seven-week cruise for him. Crossing the Equator was celebrated round the swimming-pool with much hilarity, and with ice-cream for the children and cocktails for the adults, followed by a Grand Gala Dinner to round off the day. However, it was surprising how even the most sumptuous food begins to pall after three weeks at sea. Flying fish skimmed the gentle ocean swell and several schools of dolphins leapt effortlessly from the water to keep pace with the *Himalaya's* 21 knots. One highlight of this leg of the voyage was our passing the *Arcadia*, homeward bound, and there was much dipping of ensigns and blasting of sirens to honour the Commodore in command of the P&O flagship.

We arrived in Fremantle early on the morning of Sunday 9 March which, of course, was still the Australian summer. It was in stark contrast to the cold, grey day just a few weeks earlier when we had left Tilbury. The Great Australian Bight produced its usual heavy swell, but this did nothing to deter the newly boarded Australians from sunbathing in every available spot on deck which was sheltered from the wind. The *Himalaya* spent a day each at Adelaide and Melbourne but, after five weeks at sea, we were anxious to reach Sydney and, for us, The Heads were a very welcome sight when we finally reached our destination on the morning of Tuesday 18 March.'

The *Himalaya* left Sydney once again on 21 March 1958, this time bound for Vancouver. Her first port of call was Auckland and then she steamed north for Suva where she arrived on 24 March. On her arrival at Honolulu there were great celebrations in the traditional Hawaiian style to mark her first visit, and the P&O deputy chairman, Sir Donald Anderson, was greeted by the 'Aloha Royal Hawaiian Court'; at the same time the city's civic authorities passed a special Resolution of Welcome which made it clear that P&O's Pacific enterprise met with the approval of the Hawaiians. From Honolulu the *Himalaya* steamed to Vancouver and then south to San Francisco where she docked on 10 April 1958.

By calling at the Canadian port following her stop-over at Honolulu, the *Himalaya* was able to avoid breaching US Customs law which prohibited the carriage of passengers between US ports by non-American ships. From San Francisco the *Himalaya* returned to Sydney by way of Honolulu, Suva and Auckland, finally sailing for London on 2 May 1958. On her homeward voyage, after completing her calls at the Australian ports, she left Fremantle on 9 May and steamed through the Sunda Straits to Singapore, arriving on 14 May. She then followed her traditional route home via Suez, calling at Lisbon on 30 May and arriving in Tilbury Docks early in the morning of 1 June. The *Himalaya* had undertaken the longest voyage ever by a P&O ship and had opened up new horizons for the company.

Chusan undergoes routine maintenance at Southampton.   *(P&O)*

Chapter Six

Changing Trade Patterns

In the early months of 1959 the P&O management were planning the *Chusan's* first cruise into the Pacific. It was intended that she should call at San Francisco and Vancouver before actually making a separate 15-day cruise from San Francisco to Honolulu and Vancouver, before returning to the US West Coast port. However, a complaint by Senator Warren Magnuson ensured that P&O's proposal of making Honolulu the first port of call after departing from San Francisco was ruled illegal by the US Customs Bureau. Despite the fact that all the American passengers would sleep on board the ship during a three-day stop-over it was held that this constituted a breach of the US regulations. In the event it was decided to reduce the proposed three-day stay to an overnight stop and there were no objections to this arrangement.

The *Chusan's* lengthy voyage started on 11 April 1959, when she left Tilbury for Gibraltar and Port Said, followed by her traditional route to Penang and Singapore. After leaving Singapore on 6 May she called at Manila and Hong Kong, and finally reached Yokohama on 16 May. From Japan she steamed across the Pacific Ocean to San Francisco, where she arrived on the last day of June. Her two-week cruise started the next day and it took her to Honolulu, the volcanic island of Hilo, Vancouver and back to San Francisco on the morning of 15 July. However, unlike the *Himalaya*, which had returned to the UK by way of her traditional route, the *Chusan* came home via Los Angeles, Panama, Trinidad, Las Palmas and Le Havre, finally arriving in London on 12 July 1959.

Meanwhile the *Himalaya* was making her second voyage for the 'Orient & Pacific Line's' North America - Japan service. She left London on 12 February 1959 and sailed to Australia by way of Suez and, despite a delay at Fremantle where she underwent repairs to her main engines, she arrived in Sydney on 14 March. The voyage then continued to Auckland, Suva, Honolulu, Vancouver, San Francisco and Long Beach. From there she sailed via Honolulu to Yokohama, where she suffered some minor damage whilst docking, and Kobe. From Japan she steamed to Hong Kong, Manila and Singapore, and then returned to London via Colombo, Bombay and Suez. She arrived back in Tilbury on 28 May 1959, having steamed 49,116 miles and having been away for three and a half months on the longest voyage ever undertaken by one of the company's passenger ships. Following her return to her home port, the *Himalaya* was dry docked for stabilizers to be fitted, before she sailed on her single cruise of the summer season, a 17-day voyage to the Mediterranean. During the early morning of Friday 19 June, whilst proceeding in dense fog to her berth at Venice, she went aground and her bow stuck in the muddy bottom of the Lagoon. Fortunately, after being stranded for three hours, she was refloated at 8.30 am with the assistance of tugs and with no apparent damage, the liner was able to continue the cruise as scheduled.

The *Himalaya* left London again on Friday 3 July, bound once more for Sydney and the Pacific. Just over a week into the voyage, in the early hours of Saturday 11 July whilst making her southbound transit of the Suez Canal, the vessel sheered into the canal's eastern bank and seriously damaged her port propeller. This resulted in a 24-hour delay and when she left Port Suez on 13 July her speed had to be reduced to 16 knots as she made the rest of the voyage on only one propeller. Negotiations were then conducted *en route* with the Australian government, as a result of which the Australian Navy agreed to make their dry dock facility at Garden Island available to P&O. Fortunately the *Himalaya* reached Sydney without further incident and she docked on Saturday 15 August, after a journey which lasted for six weeks. Three days later, on Tuesday 18 August, she was moved into the Captain Cook Dry Dock where there was yet more drama when strong gusts of wind blew the liner sideways as she entered the dock, bumping a tug against the dockside and snapping a seven-inch tow-rope. Once the dock had been drained it could be seen that all the blades of the port propeller had been damaged and the tailshaft was bent. Repairs to the latter took ten days and the propeller itself was replaced, at a total cost to P&O of £18,311. The *Himalaya* finally left Sydney on Saturday 29 August for the West Coast of the USA, Japan and the Far East, before returning to Sydney on 19 October. Her homeward passage to the UK was by way of her traditional route and after passing through the Suez Canal on 15 November, calling at Malta two days later, she arrived at Tilbury on 22 November, having been away for almost five months.

During the summer of 1959 the *Chusan* carried out a number of UK cruises and later in the year she made a voyage to Hong Kong via Suez, returning to London on 5 December. Earlier in the year P&O had decided that both the *Himalaya* and the *Chusan* would be completely refurbished with air-conditioning installed throughout the passenger accommodation. The contract for the *Himalaya* was secured by a Dutch shipyard, the Rotterdam Dry Dock Company, while the *Chusan* went to Harland & Wolff at Belfast.

The *Himalaya* was the first to be withdrawn from service for the refit and she arrived in Rotterdam, from London, on 27 November 1959. The *Chusan* arrived back in London from the Far East on 5 December 1959, having been delayed for over 12 hours at Gibraltar by severe gales. Both she and the Orient liner *Oronsay* had to shelter for most of the day on 1 December, and the *Braemar Castle*, which was riding out the storm in Algeciras Bay, was driven aground by the high winds. However, by 17 December *Chusan* was berthed at Queen's Island, Belfast and her refit could begin.

It was 4 February 1960 before the *Himalaya* returned to Tilbury from Rotterdam and seven days later she sailed for Sydney and San Francisco. The *Chusan's* refit was completed by 8 March 1960, when she left Belfast for London, arriving in Tilbury two days later. She sailed again on 24 March, bound for the Far East and the USA. Although the two ships retained their two classes, the air-conditioning was a great

A magnificent aerial view of the *Chusan* in the Channel.

(FotoFlite)

The *Himalaya* leaving Tilbury Docks.

improvement and absolutely essential in the US cruise market where such amenities were taken for granted.

By the early 1960s the aviation industry in both Britain and the USA had introduced jet airliners, which were now being seen as a threat by the shipowners, particularly on the North Atlantic routes. In 1948 only 240,000 people crossed the Atlantic by air and 637,000 by sea, whereas ten years later in 1958, the trend was reversed with 1,193,000 people crossing by air and 958,000 preferring the sea voyage. The picture was clear for everyone to see; between 1948 and 1958 the number of passengers using London airport had increased from 280,000 to 3·5 million, and by 1970 it was estimated that 13 million passengers would pass through the airport. In 1960 BOAC's Comet 4s were used on the London - Australia route and it was becoming clear that it would not be too long before air travel became a real threat to the passenger liners which were employed on the Far Eastern and Australian routes.

One way in which the shipping companies could counter this increased competition was to turn more and more to cruising, and P&O's fleet of liners, designed for long voyages east of Suez, were ideally suited for this role. In September 1960, during her annual refit in Southampton, the *Chusan's* dining saloons were renamed restaurants, with the first class saloon becoming the Mandarin Restaurant and the tourist class saloon the Hong Kong Restaurant. When the *Himalaya*

underwent her annual refurbishment in Tilbury between 27 October and 12 November 1960, her dining saloons were also renamed, with that in the first class becoming the Drake Restaurant and that in the tourist class the Tasman Restaurant. However, despite the fact that both vessels were catering for a large number of US passengers, the class barriers were retained for a little while longer.

The *Himalaya* left London once again on 12 November 1960, steaming by way of her traditional route to Sydney where she arrived on 13 December, and five days later she sailed on a ten-day Christmas cruise. This special cruise carried the 1,061 Australian passengers to Queen Charlotte Sound, Wellington and Akaroa and they left Sydney behind after the city had had a week of rain. The crossing of the Tasman Sea was rough, but 24 hours from New Zealand's South Island the sun came out and in Blenheim there were banners in the streets proclaiming, 'Welcome *Himalaya!*'. As the liner dropped anchor in Akaroa Harbour on Friday 23 December and her passengers went ashore, the local newspaper's headline that morning read, 'Dinkum Aussies Swarm Out From Akaroa, Invade Province.' Happily the invasion was a very friendly one and, after a successful cruise, the *Himalaya* returned to Sydney on 28 December 1960 and left for London via Suez on New Year's Eve.

Despite the changing trends in trade, the two liners continued to make their passenger/cargo voyages and one of

The *Himalaya* being dry docked at the Australian Navy's dockyard, Garden Island, Sydney, on Wednesday 19 August 1959, following her mishap in the Suez Canal whilst *en route* to Australia. *(W. Burrell)*

The *Chusan* undergoing her modernization refit at Harland & Wolff's Belfast shipyard in December 1959. *(Ernest H. Cole)*

The *Chusan* in dry dock at Southampton. *(P&O)*

Chusan's officers recalls one interesting and unusual port on a Far East voyage in January 1962 where the ship loaded a cargo of oranges before leaving Japan for Hong Kong, Singapore, Penang, Colombo, Bombay, Suez, Aden and London: 'Shimizu may be found by closely searching any large scale map of the island of Honshu, its exact location being 23 miles south-west by south from Fujiyama. The port lies in a small bay with good shelter from the sea, the drawback to this navigational attraction being that the wind invariably comes off the land. The intention was to anchor overnight and go alongside the wharf at dawn. Whilst the harbour appeared quite small for a ship with the swinging radius of *Chusan* at anchor, the entrance to the berth was even smaller and only two very small "tugs" and a pilot would be available to take the ship from the anchorage to the berth.

And so it was with a sense of adventure that at 4pm on 22 January the *Chusan* left the complacent comfort and streamlined efficiency of Yokohama, bound for the uncertain prospect of Shimizu and accompanied by all the ceremony that the Yokohama Police Band could extend. The passage round to Shimizu was uneventful and rather gave those concerned the feeling of the "calm before the storm". However, the approach to the port, which lies on the north-western side of a bay, was completed satisfactorily and *Chusan* anchored at 11pm. Apart from the biting wind, apparently coming direct from the Siberian plains, the ship settled comfortably to the routine of loading cargo. The stevedores that swarmed on board were deemed somewhat fearsome on account of their warlike appearance, all being equipped with

steel safety helmets. Japan is noted for the speed and efficiency with which cargo is worked and Shimizu must be one of the foremost ports of the country in this respect. During the ship's stay 1,060 tons were loaded in eleven hours.

With the arrival of dawn the ship prepared to weigh anchor and proceed to her berth, and the grandeur of Fujiyama, silhouetted against the crimson sky, provided a momentary distraction from the business of going alongside. The pilot was obviously impressed with the size of the *Chusan* and he began issuing rather incoherent instructions. As we approached the breakwater which formed the shelter to the quay, it was apparent that the entrance was very narrow indeed and this, combined with the strong offshore breeze, made the operation interesting, to say the least. After this hazard had been negotiated and *Chusan* was safely inside the breakwater, the final procedure was to get alongside. The appearance of two small "tugs" gave little reassurance as to their tractive powers and it was obvious that the manoeuvre would largely depend on the ship herself. The port anchor was dropped to act as a "brake" and, whilst it was helpful for getting alongside, it proved a hindrance when the time came to depart. After a while the wind was defeated and the ship was made fast alongside, secured to some rather frail bollards on a fragile looking wharf.

The time alongside was spent in loading the remainder of our cargo of oranges and arranging tours to local points of interest for the passengers. Naturally Mount Fujiyama was the main attraction, but around Shimizu are several shrines, temples and beauty spots.

As the time of departure approached, so the wharf became more and more congested with what seemed to be the majority of the population of Shimizu. Whilst Yokohama had always given an impressive welcome and farewell, with bands and even, on one occasion, a helicopter, this scene gave the impression of complete sincerity and spontaneity. The centrepiece was formed by a local college orchestra playing with abandoned gusto. The imminence of departure was emphasized by the sudden rendering of "Auld Lang Syne", smartly followed by "God Save The Queen".

The actual operation of clearing Shimizu was not without difficulty, again caused by the offshore wind, the unfortunate position of the port anchor and the fact that the only way out was by going full astern on both engines. The last of these would have been simple had it not been for the first two hindrances, which delayed and complicated the sailing.

Chusan did, eventually, depart and it was with a mild sense of relief that the voyage to Kobe was resumed and life, once again, became routine.'

The *Himalaya* was also continuing her routine voyages to and from Australia, and on 22 March 1961 she left Sydney with Richie Benaud's Australian XI for their successful summer tour of England. As Chief Officer on board the *Himalaya* in 1962 Captain Barry Thompson remembers those days: 'There was certainly a warmth of feeling as I joined *Himalaya* and, for me, she was definitely a much happier ship than the *Iberia*. The commander was Captain Howard, a funny little man, but one with a kind heart. As Chief Officer I was left to run the ship and I only went to him when I needed any assistance or advice. After two cruises from Southampton we sailed on 7 September 1962 for the

An aerial view of the *Chusan* as she leaves the Thames for Southampton and the start of a UK summer cruise season. *(FotoFlite)*

antipodes, via Le Havre, Lisbon, Trinidad, Panama and the West Coast of the USA. We arrived in Sydney on 19 October and I had some leave before we left once again a few days later. From there we sailed to Hong Kong by way of the Great Barrier Reef and we arrived in the colony on 1 November. On the following day we were joined by the *Iberia* and the *Chusan*, and it was quite a sight to see three of P&O's large liners in the port together. We made a circuit of the Pacific before returning to Sydney on Boxing Day 1962. New Year's Day was spent in Melbourne and we arrived in Tilbury on 31 January 1963, to a bitterly cold winter. I left the *Himalaya* 14 days later after a very happy voyage where everything worked like clockwork.'

More memories of the *Himalaya* are recalled, this time from a young passenger's point of view: 'I was 13 years of age when, on the morning of Saturday 26 October 1963, together with my parents, brother and sister, I embarked in the *Himalaya* for the voyage home to London from Aden, where we had lived for almost two years. We children had been counting the days for some weeks and we were quite excited as the day actually dawned. I can remember the journey from Khormaksar Airfield, where we lived, down the Maalla Strait to Steamer Point and, as we approached Tawahi, seeing the *Himalaya*'s large buff funnel slowly come into view between the buildings. She was actually moored out in the harbour, off the pier at Steamer Point, as the big liners always were, and during the two years that we had lived in Aden we had visited many of the P&O-Orient Line ships as they passed through the port. This time we were actually travelling in one ourselves and the excitement mounted as we were taken out by tender.

I can recall climbing the accommodation ladder and going into the D Deck entrance foyer where the cool air of the *Himalaya*'s air-conditioning was very welcome after the searing heat of Aden. We were shown to our cabins which were amidships on A Deck and I can remember wondering whether I would ever find my way about this enormous vessel. Our parents had a two-berth outside cabin and we children shared a three-berth room nearby, which had been made by opening the communicating doors between a single-berth and a two-berth cabin. I can remember that we had our own shower and WC and that we were on the starboard side, quite close to the gentlemen's hairdressing shop. The very "Britishness" of the ship made me feel quite at home right from the start.

We left Aden early in the afternoon of that day and once the excitement of the departure had died down we children set about exploring the ship. At that age the class barriers meant nothing to us and we regularly used to sneak surreptitiously through to the tourist class and somehow, compared with the sedate and rather "stuffy" atmosphere which prevailed in the first class, it always seemed to be bustling with activity and much more lively.

During our voyage through the Red Sea and shortly before we arrived at Port Suez, a stowaway was found by the Chief Steward in the A Deck foyer who, apparently, had been on board since the ship left Bombay some six days previously. He was transferred to the *Cathay* which was bound for the Far East, in order that he could be returned to Malaya, which was where he had originally come from. He was taken over to the other ship by the *Himalaya's* motor boat and a lot of passengers, myself included, lined the ship's rail to watch the transfer take place. Once the motor boat was back and hoisted into the davits, the *Himalaya* was soon under way again and heading for the Suez Canal.

I can also recall that during our transit of the Suez Canal an elderly first class passenger died and she was buried at sea after we had left Port Said. The funeral service was held at 4.30pm on the afternoon of 30 October and it was conducted by the *Himalaya's* master, Captain P. G. Lawrence.

I remember entering the children's fancy dress competition and, having decided to enter as a chef, going down through the Mandarin Restaurant into the kitchens and food preparation areas, where one of the *Himalaya's* cooks fitted me up with his working clothes and accoutrements and, for good measure, a false moustache.

After calling at Naples and Marseilles, our final stop was Gibraltar where we stayed for less than five hours. We anchored off the South Mole in Algeciras Bay and I can remember being ferried ashore by tender. However, with such a short stay and with the ship being anchored so far from the shore, I did not enjoy my time in Gib as I was unable to shake off the feeling that we were bound to miss the ship. I had visions of turning up for the boat back only to see the *Himalaya* steaming west towards the Atlantic Ocean.

Fortunately my fears were unfounded and we finally arrived in Tilbury early on the morning of Friday 8 November 1963, which was a very blustery day and the one thing which sticks in my mind is of looking out of our cabin porthole to see large, fluffy white clouds, racing across the skies. This was a strange phenomenon for, having lived in Aden for nearly two years, we had hardly ever seen a cloud at all. It left an indelible memory of the return to Tilbury and the end of our voyage home in the *Himalaya*.'

On her return to London the *Himalaya* underwent a refit and refurbishment to adapt her further for the ever growing leisure industry and her cruising role, but it was also a reminder that she was ageing and that she was no longer the pride of the P&O fleet.

As 1963 drew to a close, the *Chusan* was berthed at No 9 shed, King George V Docks in London when, on the evening of Wednesday 4 December, she suffered fire damage in her insulated refrigeration spaces. Fortunately, with the fire brigade quickly on the scene a serious conflagration was avoided and she was able to sail for Japan 12 days later.

As the mid-1960s approached, both the *Chusan* and the *Himalaya* were still making their traditional liner voyages to the Far East and Australia respectively, but these were becoming fewer and it would not be long before both ships would need a new role.

The *Himalaya* arrives in Southampton at the end of a cruise.

(F. R. Sherlock)

The *Chusan* moored off Steamer Point, Aden, in the late 1950s. Before the closure of the Suez Canal all the eastbound mailships called at Aden on both the outward and homeward legs of their voyages. *(Duncan Smedley)*

The *Chusan* at Southampton on 30 July 1971, shortly before leaving the port on a two-week cruise which had actually started at Amsterdam three days earlier. She returned to Amsterdam on 11 August. *(Don Smith)*

Making a lot of black smoke, the *Chusan* passes Hythe Pier in Southampton Water on 15 April 1972, as she leaves for a 23-day cruise to the Caribbean. *(Don Smith)*

A fine aerial view of the *Himalaya* in the Thames estuary.

Chapter Seven

Troubled Times

Upon her arrival at Tilbury on 8 November 1963, the *Himalaya* was taken over by R. H. Green & Silley Weir for her annual overhaul and for conversion into a one-class ship. By now the class barriers were an outmoded idea, reminiscent of Victorian and Edwardian society, and demands for their removal had been strong, particularly on the Australian and Pacific trade routes. During the refurbishment the children's playroom at the forward end of the Promenade Deck was retained while the two small lounges on either side of the main staircase became the Hillary and Tensing Rooms. The main first class lounge became the Everest Room, and the old first class Verandah Café was completely refitted on the port side to create the Overland Bar, whilst the starboard side was converted for use as a cinema with a central screen and seating for 140 passengers. On B Deck the former tourist class ballroom was split up to create two separate rooms, with the port side becoming the Yeti Tavern, complete with juke box. The starboard side was now called the Cascade Room. At the after end of C Deck the tourist class Smoking Room became the Boot & Piton and what had been the tourist class children's nursery was turned into the after playground. At the after end of D Deck the old tourist class lounge became the John Hunt Room, and overall the ship's passenger capacity was increased from 1,136 to 1,416 with the provision of additional berths in what had been single-berth cabins on A Deck, and the larger two-berth rooms on B Deck.

Following her conversion, the *Himalaya's* first voyage from Tilbury to Sydney, via Suez, started on 21 November 1963 and she arrived in Sydney 30 days later on 21 December. On Christmas Eve that year she made her first cruise as a one-class ship, a seven-day voyage across the Tasman Sea to Auckland and back returning to Sydney on New Year's Eve and leaving for London, via Suez, two days later.

Meanwhile in July 1963, after making her usual voyage from London to the Far East, the *Chusan* left Singapore bound for Australia for the first time in her career. After calling at Fremantle on 3 July, she steamed on to Adelaide and Melbourne before arriving in Sydney on 10 July. It was her introduction to the antipodes and from Sydney she made a three-week cruise to New Zealand and into the Pacific before leaving Australia on 8 August for Singapore and home, via Suez.

Although the *Chusan* remained a two-class ship, in keeping with modern trends, the public rooms were all renamed to reflect the origin of the *Chusan's* name. The first class lounge became the Pagoda Room, the dancing space the Neptune Ballroom, and at the after end of the Promenade Deck the Verandah Café became the Marco Polo Room. In the tourist class section the lounge was named the Cathay Lounge, the Smoking Room became the Dragon Bar and the ballroom became the Ocean Room.

However, the retention of the two classes did cause problems and Captain 'Dickie' Firth, who was the *Chusan's* Staff Captain for three years between 1964 and 1966 recalls some of the difficulties: 'Management decreed that the first and tourist class passengers should not mix, which meant two church services on a Sunday, two Santa Clauses at Christmas and, for me, two duckings when we "crossed the line". It was all rather futile and one could not be rude or harsh with a paying customer who happened to wander into the other class. It was also very difficult to find a neutral area for the various charity fundraising events to which passengers of both classes were invited. Passengers in both the first and the tourist classes complained and we told them to write to Head Office. Obviously a lot of them did and our Managing Director came on board in Madeira for the voyage home. He discussed the problem with me and, fortunately, the "no fraternization" policy was relaxed.

On a happier note I remember the first leg of our world voyage of early 1964, which was a normal Far East voyage. Just before departure I had worked out an entertainment programme, but the "old man" told me to alter the "Fancy Dress Night" to "Surprise Night", but he wouldn't tell me what he had in mind. However, a couple of days before the big event the "old man" let me in on the secret. We were going to have a Roman Festival and as he said, "They've paid a lot of money to come with us, the company can afford to lose a few sheets and bath towels". Anyway the evening was a howling success and all our regulars, mainly hardbitten tea- and rubber-planters, enjoyed themselves immensely. Mind you it put pressure on the entertainment staff who, in those days, consisted of myself, a sports deck quartermaster and a social hostess. However, with the help of some old navigation charts, we managed to transform the ballroom into quite a passable Roman Forum. The success of this event led to a number of "theme nights", some of which can be seen on P&O's modern cruise ships and although we never repeated the Roman Festival, we had "Italian Night", "London Night" and, once into Far Eastern waters, "Chinese Night".

From our regular passengers of those days two "characters" come to mind. The first was a charming and, apparently, well-connected lady of some 17 or 18 stones, with a wonderful sense of fun. On fancy dress night she would always don a tutu and come along as "Fairy Snow", and she would dust the "old man" and the other judges liberally with talcum powder at the end of the parade. The second was a very elegant, tall and slim lady, with a perfect Edwardian buffed-up hairstyle and a beautiful period evening dress. She would tuck a dozen pairs of panties over her bosom and come along as a "chest of drawers". She always brought the house down, but the "old man", who was a bit of a prude, whispered to me, "that's out for a start". Needless to say she won first prize to the acclaim of all, except one.

Another first in *Chusan* was our "Country Fayre" which we put on for a little light relief during the long crossing from Honolulu to Yokohama, and it was very popular with the American passengers. We used to pray that the chosen day was fine and dry as it entailed a lot of work and organization to set it up. All available hands used to turn out to set up the

The *Chusan* alongside No 9 shed in King George V Dock, London, on 7 March 1964. She sailed the following day for Kobe. *(Ambrose Greenway)*

Below: The *Himalaya* turning off Circular Quay, Sydney, on 24 March 1965. She was leaving on a cruise to Japan, Hong Kong and Manila, and she returned to Sydney on 23 April 1965.

(Ambrose Greenway)

Himalaya arrives in Sydney in 1965. In the background the city's now famous Opera House is still under construction.

(Ambrose Greenway)

The *Himalaya* about to pass under Sydney Harbour Bridge in the mid-1960s. *(Ambrose Greenway)*

The *Himalaya* at Sydney.

(*Ambrose Greenway*)

stalls and side-shows, and to provide the entertainment which often went on into the early hours of the following morning. All the usual fairground events were there; smash the crockery, coconut shies, hoop-la, darts, bobbing for apples, fortune tellers, and most of us dressed for the occasion, with the Chief Engineer suitably attired as the "vicar" and a stenographer as a Sally Anne, collecting for seamen's charities. The end result was a happy ship's company and a happy ship. As can be imagined we built up a sizeable wardrobe of "props" for the various events.

Our arrivals at the Japanese ports of Kobe and Yokohama were always very colourful for the passengers, with the local tourist board providing a beauty queen, together with chaperons and hangers-on. There were always long speeches of welcome from the Mayor, and the Captain was usually presented with a Japanese doll in a glass case. For some reason I, as Staff Captain, was presented with a bunch of flowers.'

In May 1964, whilst the *Chusan* was steaming across the Pacific, two days out from Honolulu *en route* for Yokohama, a loss of power was noticed in the starboard high-pressure turbine. The technical details are described by Norman Pound, who was one of the ship's senior engineers: 'In order to keep up our speed and schedule the bled steam (IP inlet and IP second expansion) valves were closed in to two turns and the vapour from the fresh water evaporator was fed to the first LP heater. With the vapour valve to the port distiller opened two turns, this gave increased revolutions.

However, after leaving Yokohama on 18 May for Kobe, a further loss of power was apparent - the mean revolutions being 127 at 20/21 nozzles - and after Kobe power continued to deteriorate. Upon our arrival at Hong Kong on 22 May the starboard engine was compounded and the high-pressure turbine was bypassed. When the turbine covers were removed a great deal of damage to the turbine blades was found, but as it was impossible to carry out permanent repairs we continued the voyage at reduced soeed. The exhaust outlet from the high-pressure turbine was not blanked off as we had great difficulty in removing the necessary bolts from the bellows piece. However, on passage from Hong Kong to Manila the bellows piece split and upon our arrival at the Philippines' capital we effected a repair by welding a patch. At Singapore, on 29 May, the bellows piece was cut out and blanks were fitted to the pipe.' Fortunately the remainder of the voyage passed without any additional problems and upon her arrival in London on 21 June the high-pressure turbine could be opened and permanent repairs were carried out.

At 8.30pm on Monday 7 September 1964, as the *Himalaya* lay alongside No 33 shed at Tilbury Docks between voyages, thick, black, oily smoke was seen belching from her funnel and the alarm was raised. Soot deposits in the smoke uptake shafts had caught fire and it took the Essex Fire Brigade two hours to extinguish the blaze, but damage was minimal and she was able to sail for Australia four days later on 11 September.

The *Chusan* in the Solent during the 1960s.
(F. R. Sherlock)

By the mid-1960s the number of travellers who were making their journeys by air was steadily increasing and this was having a marked effect on the Far East and Australian shipping routes. In 1966 Lord Simon, a former director of P&O, sounded a warning when he announced: 'Passenger ships are on the way out. Except for a few cruise liners, most ships will be carrying cargo in ten years time. Businessmen will take advantage of mammoth jet aircraft.' However, he ended his speech by saying that, '...cruising and other forms of tourism will increase.' When asked for his comments the General Manager of P&O's Passenger Services replied: 'What we have to do is find ways of using passenger ships profitably and this we intend to do. We think that a passenger ship is an end in itself rather than a means of transportation and, far from deteriorating, the popularity of passenger ships has been increasing over certain routes in recent years, particularly over Pacific routes.'

It was clear that the crisis which the growth of air travel had brought to the Atlantic shipping lanes was about to hit the traditional routes between London and Sydney, and South-East Asia. Unknown to anyone at the time was the fact that the end of the liner voyage would be hastened by political events in the Middle East.

The *Himalaya* steams down the Solent on 15 July 1967, bound for a two-week Mediterranean cruise. *(Ambrose Greenway)*

Chapter Eight

The Final Years

On Thursday 7 April 1966 the *Chusan* left Southampton for Australia via Lisbon and Panama. Eight days later she arrived in Bermuda with several injured passengers and a slightly damaged bow as a result of a severe storm in mid-Atlantic between the Azores and Bermuda. However, after taking on fuel and water she was able to leave for Port Everglades, Nassau, Panama and Sydney.

Five months later the *Himalaya* was in the news when, at 10.40am on Wednesday 28 September 1966, whilst she was berthed alongside No 32 shed in Tilbury Docks, a fire broke out near the engine-room. Fortunately it was quickly extinguished and none of the cargo which had been loaded was damaged. Two days later the *Himalaya* left London for Suez and Australia. The *Himalaya's* next Pacific voyage started from Tilbury on 23 December 1966 and she steamed into the Mediterranean and anchored off Piraeus six days later, where she embarked Greek migrants bound for Australia. After arriving in Sydney on 23 January 1967 she made a short seven-day cruise to Wellington and back. However, on the last day of the cruise she ran into cyclone 'Dinah' which had been battering much of the Queensland coast with 100mph winds for two days, leaving a trail of havoc as it tore the roofs off hundreds of homes. As the storm moved south-south-east at just over ten miles an hour, the *Himalaya* was pounded by huge seas, and as one enormous wave smashed into the vessel, passengers, tables, chairs and equipment in the ballroom were piled into a jumbled heap. The force of the wave broke one and a half inch porthole glass and buckled steel deadlights. Twelve passengers were treated for injuries, which were mainly cuts and bruises and, although it had been only a short cruise, it was not one which would be forgotten by those on board. On 2 February the *Himalaya* left for London by way of

Brisbane, Hong Kong, Singapore, Bombay, Aden, Suez and Naples, and she arrived in Tilbury on 10 March. Thirteen days later she left London once again and made a similar round voyage to Australia, with a short cruise from Sydney to Wellington, sailing from Sydney again for London on 4 May 1967. However, her voyage home this time was more direct and after calling at the traditional Australian ports she steamed to Colombo, Bombay and Aden. She made her final transit of the Suez Canal on 25/26 May at a time of great diplomatic tension in the Middle East. On 19 May Egypt had ordered that the UN peace-keeping force on the border with Israel be removed and three days later had closed the Straits of Tiran to Israeli shipping. On 5 June 1967, as the *Himalaya* docked at Tilbury, the Six-Day War in the Middle East broke out and for the second time in eleven years the Suez Canal was closed, this time for eight years.

The political problems in the Middle East did not affect the *Chusan* during the summer of 1967 for, after arriving in Southampton on 9 April and undergoing her annual overhaul, she started a series of 13 UK cruises. Unfortunately during the sixth cruise she encountered mechanical problems. She had left Southampton on the afternoon of 15 July bound for Lisbon, Venice and Cadiz, and she was due back at Southampton early on the morning of 30 July. All went well for most of the voyage and she left Cadiz on 28 July as scheduled. However, at about 3.30pm on Saturday 29 July, when she was some nine miles off Ushant, she lost all power and was left drifting helplessly. The first indications of trouble came when a signal was received at Lands End as follows: '*Chusan* drifting nine miles 4° off Creach Point, Ushant, all boiler feed water gone. First possibility of steam 6am. Tug required to stand by soonest. Not under command.'

On 10 October 1969 the *Himalaya* left Tilbury for the last time. It also marked the transfer of P&O's passenger ship operations from London to Southampton. *(P&O)*

The *Himalaya* anchored off Noumea on 14 July 1969, during a cruise from Sydney.
(Daryl Stevens)

The *Chusan* leaves Cape Town on 11 December 1971 for a 25-day cruise to South America.
(Captain J. L. Chapman)

The *Chusan* at Cape Town. *(J. K. Byass)*

The *Himalaya* in Canadian waters during early 1972.
(J. K. Byass)

2 May 1973, and the *Chusan* is laid up at Southampton's 101 berth before her final departure to the shipbreakers.
(R. Catterall)

As it happened the *Himalaya* had left Malaga on 27 July, to return to Southampton after a two-week Mediterranean cruise, and she was ordered to stand by the helpless *Chusan*. For 15 hours the *Chusan's* engineers worked to raise steam once again and at 6.30am on 31 July she was able to signal: '*Chusan* under way, bound for Southampton'. She finally arrived back alongside 107 berth at Southampton Docks at 4.30pm the same day, over 24 hours behind schedule.

Although the *Chusan* completed her summer cruise programme, the problems with her boilers recurred in December 1967, even though she had undergone a thorough, three-week long overhaul in November. During the afternoon of Saturday 9 December 1967, the *Chusan* left Southampton for Sydney via Panama and Honolulu, but less than 12 hours out of the port she developed boiler trouble and was forced to turn back. In the event she was able to put to sea again on Monday 11 December, just 48 hours behind schedule. Fortunately the remainder of the voyage was completed without encountering any further problems and the liner arrived in Sydney on 26 January 1968.

By the summer of 1969, P&O were preparing to move the centre of their passenger ship operations, and the terminal port for the ships, from Tilbury to Southampton. The company had, in fact, moved to Tilbury from Southampton in June 1903 and for 66 years the port had been the company's 'second home'. However, during the 1960s there had been some significant changes to the long established trade patterns and the move was essential in order to reduce voyage times by 24 hours. In addition, the company's two largest ships, *Canberra* and *Oriana*, with their gross tonnage of over 40,000 and their deep draughts, were unable to use Tilbury and they had been based in Southampton since the early 1960s.

In fact, since January 1966 the *Chusan* had only used Tilbury on one occasion, and the *Himalaya* was sailing from Southampton on almost all her cruise departures, so moving the company's administrative centre to the Hampshire port made sense. It was the *Himalaya* that made the company's last departure from Tilbury when, on 10 October 1969, she left the Passenger Landing Stage for the last time, at the start of a voyage to Sydney via Lisbon, Las Palmas, Cape Town and

Left and below: On Saturday 12 May 1973 the *Chusan* left Southampton for the last time - bound for Kaohsiung and the shipbreakers' yard.
(John J. Callis)

Durban. The event had not gone unheralded and, in fact, a special luncheon had been held on board the previous day.

However, even this move could not disguise the economic facts and the passenger lists for liner voyages between the UK and Australian and Far Eastern ports were dwindling every year. In February 1970 the *Chusan* bade farewell to a port which had been a traditional call for P&O passenger ships for over 140 years, when she made the last scheduled stop at Bombay. To mark the occasion Vice-Admiral S. N. Nanda of the Indian Navy made an official visit to the ship, and during the vessel's two-day stay in Bombay the Prince of Wales Seamen's Club presented Captain R. B. Nowell with a plaque for P&O's historic records. When the *Chusan* left Bombay on the morning of 8 February 1970 to continue her voyage to Sydney, she was played out by the Indian Navy band, who gave a fine performance.

Two days later, on 10 February, the *Chusan* called at Colombo and berthed alongside the Queen Elizabeth Quay. This was the first time that a large passenger liner had been berthed alongside and not in the stream as was the normal practice, but as there was a strike of port workers, including

the crews of motor launches who manned the ship to shore traffic, it was the best solution. Unfortunately this did not set a precedent for it was the *Chusan's* penultimate visit to the port. She called at Colombo for the last time during her homeward voyage on 22 March 1970, thus ending a P&O passenger service to and from Ceylon (Sri Lanka), which had lasted for well over a century.

On 9 April 1970, when the *Himalaya* steamed into Kobe, she opened the Japanese port's new passenger ship terminal which was situated on Pier 4, and which was reached by an elongated highway system linking the massive Kobe Ohashi Grand Bridge with the waterfront and a man-made island and container port. The new terminal was a three-storey structure with cargo facilities on the first floor, and passenger facilities on the second and third floors. The opening ceremony took the form of a Shinto religious ceremony and it was attended by government representatives, civic dignitaries, Captain J. W. Terry, the *Himalaya's* master, and a number of passengers who were on board for the month-long cruise which had started at Sydney on 29 March 1970.

By now the 'writing was on the wall' as BOAC took

delivery of its first Boeing 747 jet airliners. Spanning 195ft and weighing 325 tons, the Boeing 747 could carry 404 passengers at 550mph for some 5,000 miles. In addition to this formidable competition came sharp rises in the price of oil fuel, and with the continued closure of the Suez Canal it was absolutely clear that the days of the traditional liner voyage were over and that the passenger ships of the P&O would have to turn to the leisure industry in order to remain viable. By the late 1960s the *Himalaya* was making only two round voyages to Australia each year and these were essentially in order to position the vessel for either the UK or the Australian cruise markets. Likewise the *Chusan* spent a greater part of the year cruising from Sydney or from Southampton. However, although the passenger liners were turning more and more to the cruise markets, the demand for such holidays was not increasing dramatically.

Despite these problems the two ships continued to provide an excellent service to passengers. The *Himalaya* spent much of the year cruising in Australian waters, and Daryl Stevens of Cooloongup, Western Australia, describes the atmosphere on board in those days: 'To the Australian cruise passenger the *Himalaya* was a special ship and her cruises were always well patronized, with some "Aussies" cruising so many times each year that they regarded her as a second home. Whilst cruising from Sydney she would use the terminals at Circular Quay and No 21 Pyrmont. My favourite departures were from Circular Quay where we were often treated to the music of the Australian Navy's band from HMAS *Penguin*. They always played "Now Is The Hour" and it was a sentimental favourite with the passengers who threw thousands of paper streamers to relatives and friends in the terminal and, in their turn, the crowds in the terminal threw streamers back onto the decks of the *Himalaya*. It was all very exciting and one would have thought that the goodbyes were for ever and not just for South Pacific cruises.

On the first morning at sea "Good Morning" news sheets were delivered to cabins in plenty of time to plan one's day and the activities included "walk a mile" sessions, deck sports tournaments, card meetings, navigation bridge visits, movies and, of course, the inevitable bingo. One of my particular favourites was the "greasy pole" contest in the swimming-pool. In the evening there was dancing, cabaret and discos and, for the drinkers, there were the usual gathering points which were the Boot & Piton and the pool bar. For those who just wished to relax there was the Everest Lounge on the Promenade Deck.

My sister, Gail, was invited to a "bathers and pyjamas" party at the pool bar one evening and, unknown to her, the penalty for arriving "incorrectly dressed" was an immediate dunking in the pool. In the event, having arrived in a suntop and slacks, she was immediately thrown into the pool. However, she later arrived in the correct attire and she didn't leave the party until 2.30am the next morning.

I can remember during a Tahitian Cruise an elderly passenger died and the burial service was held at sea on the weather deck, right outside the Boot & Piton and, at the appropriate moment, as the deceased was about to be committed to the deep, the pianist struck up Frank Sinatra's "My Way". He timed it perfectly to coincide with the conclusion of the service and then, without a single break, he continued with the tune which he had originally been playing.

At the time it really fitted the atmosphere of the occasion.

In those days the big cruise ships could not berth alongside in Noumea and we always anchored out and went ashore in the ship's boats. I can remember that on the quay where we landed there used to be an eccentric English gentleman who ran his own information booth for the benefit of the Australian passengers. I can still remember the look of horror on one lady's face when, after enquiring after the nearest toilet, she was directed to the communal building nearby which accommodated everyone, including pets.

The service on board the *Himalaya* was second to none and I recall one of our cabin stewards, Brian "Hubby" Husband, who always woke us very early in the morning with a cheerful greeting. No matter how we tried to deter him from waking us he always arrived at the same time with our morning tea. "Hubby" was a fine example of the efficient P&O cabin steward which one came to expect in the 1960s and 1970s. There was always such a wonderful atmosphere on board the *Himalaya* which the modern cruise ships, however well appointed, just cannot match.'

On 19 June 1970, the *Chusan* left Southampton for a 13-night cruise to Narvik and Copenhagen, calling first at Amsterdam on 20 June. It was the first of four Amsterdam-based cruises which were aimed at the Continental market and her arrival marked the official opening of a new £2 million passenger terminal. On her arrival at Amsterdam early in the morning the *Chusan*, which was dressed overall, was escorted to her berth by a fleet of tugs, while fireboats played their hoses in salute. On the quayside crowds greeted the P&O liner whilst the Amsterdam Police Band played her in. Soon after she had been securely berthed alongside, the city's Burgomaster arrived and, together with Captain E. Snowden of the *Chusan*, he performed the opening ceremony. It was clear from the speeches made that day that P&O considered Amsterdam to be an ideal location for a cruise terminal and that the use of the port was an experiment which it was hoped would secure the immediate future for the *Chusan*.

When the cruises ended on 16 August 1970, the *Chusan* started her summer season from Southampton and in the following month she was one of 70 merchant ships which took part in the NATO maritime exercise, 'Northern Wedding'. In all some 200 naval and merchant ships participated and passengers on one Mediterranean cruise were treated to the spectacle of a Naval officer being winched onto the *Chusan's* deck from a Wessex helicopter from Portland, in order that procedures involving the naval control of shipping could be exercised.

The *Chusan's* final UK cruise during the 1970 season was a three-week Christmas and New Year voyage to the West Indies, starting on 19 December and arriving back in Southampton on 9 January 1971. Then, after her annual overhaul, she left Southampton for Sydney via Panama, the US West Coast and Auckland. She left the New Zealand port on 7 March to make the voyage across the Tasman Sea, but two days into the crossing an elderly passenger suffered a serious leg injury and a radio message was sent asking for assistance. That same day an RAAF aircraft took off to parachute much needed drugs and medical instruments to the *Chusan*, which was 500 miles east of Sydney. Fortunately everything went as planned and the liner's two doctors were

The *Himalaya's* final departure from Southampton on 18 May 1974. It was her last line voyage from the UK to Sydney via Cape Town. *(R. Moody)*

able to carry out an operation, before the patient was landed at Sydney the following day. On the voyage home from Sydney the *Chusan* called at Darwin on 19 March, and after visiting both Hong Kong and Singapore she returned to Southampton via Cape Town. During the summer of 1971 she once again used Amsterdam as her cruising base and her series of eight cruises was completed on 19 September 1971. On 11 July, whilst the *Chusan* was at Southampton between cruises, thick black smoke belching from the ship's funnel caused the alarm to be raised, and the city's fire brigade took over an hour to extinguish a fire in the funnel uptakes. With temperatures that day of almost 90°F a number of firemen were treated for heat exhaustion, but there was no serious damage on the ship and *Chusan* was able to sail for Amsterdam on 16 July 1971.

One member of her ship's company, a Woman Assistant Purser, recalls her time on board the *Chusan*: 'I will always be thankful that the first ship which I joined as a Woman Assistant Purser was the *Chusan* as she was always considered to be a happy ship, and the 18 months I spent in her was, I think, the happiest time of my career.

I joined the ship at Southampton on 19 September 1971 and my first duties were on the Bureau Counter. We sailed on 2 October for a charter voyage with South African passengers who were returning home by way of New York, Nassau, Panama, the US West Coast, Japan, Hong Kong, Singapore and Colombo. The first few days were rather choppy and, as a newcomer, I was horrified when I spilt printing fluid on my brand new Hardy Amies uniform evening dress. However, I soon settled in and, although we were always busy, it was enjoyable work.

We arrived in Yokohama on 12 November and it had been decided that all the passengers would travel overland from that city to Kobe, where they would rejoin the ship. This gave us a break from the pressure of passengers, which was very welcome on such a long voyage, but it was strange to be sailing without any passengers on board - it made the *Chusan* feel almost like a "ghost ship". In those days all officers and crew members joined and left the ship only when she returned to the UK and I found that giving 100 per cent, day after day for six months, was very exhausting. Therefore the break was very welcome, both to me and my colleagues.

The charter voyage ended at Cape Town on 9 December 1971 and following this the *Chusan* spent some weeks cruising from the port, calling at such places as Lourenco Marques (Maputo), Luanda, Beira, the Seychelles, Mauritius, Rio de Janeiro, Montevideo, Buenos Aires and even passing close to Tristan da Cunha.

We finally arrived back in Southampton on 13 March 1972, and that summer we cruised to the West Indies, Scandinavia and the Atlantic Isles. Some of the cruises started and finished at Amsterdam and two Dutch Women Assistant Pursers embarked for the benefit of passengers from that country. They were exceptional with their language ability, but it was time-consuming and rather annoying to have to make announcements in two different languages. It is a shame that these cruises were not more successful, for they were very enjoyable. The *Chusan* had a reputation as a friendly, happy ship which was well justified, and I remember her with great affection.'

Another member of the ship's company who would agree with that assessment of the *Chusan* is the ex-Staff Captain, Joe Chapman, who met his future wife, Lilias, on board during the first cruise from Cape Town to Durban, Lourenco Marques and Beira. The couple announced their engagement on board and they held a 'reception' in the ship whilst the *Chusan* was at Durban. One notable passenger during the South African cruise programme was the surgeon, Professor Christian Barnard, who pioneered heart transplant surgery and who, for the less squeamish passengers, gave illustrated lectures on heart transplants.

It was during the *Chusan's* first cruise from Southampton in 1972 that the vessel was involved in a collision which, fortunately, was not serious. She had left Southampton on 30 March for a two-week cruise to Majorca, Tangier, Madeira, Gibraltar and Lisbon and at just before 7am on Tuesday 4 April she had left Palma, Majorca, bound for Tangier. Although the weather was calm that day, the harbour was blanketed in dense fog and as the *Chusan* cleared the outer breakwater she was in collision with the Spanish postal steamer *Mallorca* which was entering harbour. Fortunately there were no casualties and the *Chusan* suffered only minor damage to her forepeak, while the Spanish vessel was damaged to her port side by the navigating bridge, where steel plates were torn back. The *Chusan* continued her cruise which terminated at Southampton on 14 April 1972.

Unfortunately, despite the *Chusan's* popularity with both passengers and crew members, P&O were finding it impossible to operate nine large passenger liners with a total gross tonnage of 285,000, in a limited cruising market. In February 1972 they had announced that the *Iberia* was to be withdrawn from service and in early April 1972 they also purchased a partially constructed cruise ship which was to be the *Spirit of London*. It was clear that the company had abandoned any ideas of trying to compete with jet aircraft on the traditional routes to the Far East and Australia and that they were going to concentrate on cruising.

On 27 April 1972 came the announcement that P&O were withdrawing three of their oldest ships from service, the *Chusan*, the *Orcades* and the *Oronsay*. It was clear that the end was near for both the *Chusan* and the *Orcades* for they were omitted from the P&O brochures for 1973, while the

Oronsay was given a reprieve which would take her through to 1975. The *Chusan's* date for withdrawal was set for March 1973. These were painful times for people employed on the ships, but there was no choice as the company had to continue its policy of reducing the line voyages and concentrating on its established and expanding cruise market. It was sad to see these great names about to disappear, especially for those who served in them, but it was a realistic decision.

The *Chusan's* 1972 cruising season was based on both Southampton and Amsterdam and she visited all the traditional ports in the Mediterranean, the Atlantic Isles, Scandinavia and the West Indies. On 13 September 1972 she left Southampton for her final voyage to Australia by way of Cape Town and on her return to the South African port on 3 December she made a series of five cruises similar to the programme which she had carried out the previous year.

The *Chusan* left Cape Town for the last time on 9 March 1973 and, after calling at Dakar on 17 March, she arrived in Tenerife two days later. For British passengers who were loyal devotees of the *Chusan* there was a last chance to travel in the ship when P&O arranged a seven-night fly-cruise, leaving Gatwick on Saturday 17 March on a flight to join the ship at Tenerife. They embarked at noon on Monday 19 March and during the last cruise home called at Las Palmas, Lanzarote, Madeira and Lisbon, before arriving at Southampton on the morning of Monday 26 March 1973. Following this the *Chusan* made a seven-day trip from Rotterdam to Lisbon on 28 March. She disembarked passengers for the last time in the Dutch port on 4 April 1973, and she returned to Southampton the following day when she was laid up at 101 berth in the Western Docks.

The *Chusan* left Southampton for the last time on Saturday 12 May 1973 on a long, six-week voyage which would end at the shipbreakers' yard in Kaohsiung. It was a fine sunny day as the *Chusan*, manned only by a skeleton crew, steamed down Southampton Water and through the Needles Channel. She made her first stop at Dakar six days later and on Thursday 31 May she called at Durban for bunkers. On Wednesday 13 June she anchored in Singapore's Outer Roads and four days later she arrived in Hong Kong where she remained for just over a week. On Monday 25 June she left the colony for the final leg of her voyage east across the South China Sea to Kaohsiung where she arrived early on the morning of Saturday 30 June 1973, and where she was handed over to the shipbreakers.

Meanwhile, for the *Himalaya*, it was business as usual and after leaving Southampton for Sydney on 19 May 1972, the liner spent the remainder of the year cruising from the Australian port. On 19 August that year the vessel collided with the wharf whilst going alongside at Tonga and, although the damage to her starboard shell plating was not serious, it was clear that she would have to be dry docked. However, after undergoing a survey, it was decided that the repairs could wait until the liner returned to Southampton, which was on 20 March 1973 when she was dry docked for a thorough overhaul. Following this the *Himalaya* made two cruises from Southampton before leaving for Australia once again on 18 May. Again the remainder of the year was spent cruising from Sydney and she did not return to Southampton until 20 March 1974 when she underwent her final overhaul.

On Friday 18 October 1974, with her paying-off pennant flying and fire tenders wishing her farewell, the *Himalaya* left Sydney for her last cruise which would end at Hong Kong, followed by her final voyage to the Kaohsiung shipbreakers' yard where she arrived on the morning of 28 November 1974.

(P&O)

Following this she made three cruises from her home port, the first two into the Mediterranean, with the third being a 'farewell' cruise of just two nights across to Amsterdam and back, for even before the cruise programme had finished P&O announced that, on completion of her Australian cruise season in October 1974, the *Himalaya* was to be withdrawn from service. This came as no surprise since the company had just announced that they were negotiating to buy Princess Cruises, the US-based cruise company. This acquisition, together with the *Spirit of London*, which was soon to be renamed *Sun Princess*, gave P&O three purpose-built cruise ships and it was clear that the older passenger/cargo liners would be withdrawn. It was also announced that P&O's cruises from Australia would be carried out by the *Oriana* and the *Oronsay*, supplemented by the *Arcadia* which was being transferred from the West Coast of the USA when the *Himalaya* was withdrawn.

The *Himalaya* left Southampton for the last time on 18 May 1974 on a line voyage to Sydney by way of Lisbon, Casablanca, Dakar, Cape Town, Durban, Fremantle, Adelaide and Melbourne, arriving at her destination on 21 June 1974. She then made a series of eight cruises from Sydney, mainly to Pacific Island ports as well as Brisbane, Newcastle (NSW) and, on 8 October 1974, Auckland. Her last full cruise ended in Sydney at 3.35pm on 17 October 1974. The season had been a resounding success with hundreds of passengers eager to make a farewell cruise aboard the *Himalaya*.

Her final cruise was an eleven-day, one-way voyage from Sydney to Hong Kong for which she was fully booked. This last, sad trip began at 3.35pm on Friday 18 October 1974 when the last of the *Himalaya's* mooring ropes were let go as she broke her 25-year link with the port. As the grand old lady pulled away from the Overseas Passenger Terminal, tugs dressed overall in bunting nudged her out into the harbour while two police launches waited ready to escort her. Handkerchiefs waved by the many hundreds of loyal *Himalaya* fans who were lining Circular Quay blew in the breeze and naval vessels, ferries and hundreds of small craft saluted the ship with whistles and hooters as she slowly turned under Sydney Harbour Bridge. Then, as she moved down harbour, with her 150-ft, red, white and blue paying-off pennant flying proudly, the *Himalaya* replied with long blasts on her siren. Such was the interest among the residents of Sydney that the Department of Transport put on a special ferry to follow the ship out to Sydney Heads.

At 1.50am on Sunday 20 October she arrived in Brisbane, and after a stay of just over nine hours she was given a rousing send-off as hundreds of people lined Hamilton Wharf to see her steam down the river for the last time. As she finally left Australia, messages of goodwill poured into the ship from all parts of the country, for the ship had actually brought many families from Britain to their new homes in Australia and it was the end of a sentimental link.

At 7.05am on Tuesday 29 October the *Himalaya* made a three-hour call at Manila and two days later, at 7.59am on Thursday 31 October, the cruise ended at Hong Kong where hundreds of tearful passengers disembarked for the last time. Four days later the majority of the crew were signed off and flown home to the UK and to India, leaving only Captain J. W. Terry, 12 of his officers and 26 crew members on board.

Like the *Chusan* the *Himalaya* had been sold to Taiwanese shipbreakers and she left Hong Kong for her final voyage at 4pm on 26 November. The last entry in her official log for Thursday 28 November 1974 reads: 'This day it is noted that arrival at the breakers' yard, Kaohsiung, was made at 9.58am'. And so she had finally come to the end of her 25-year career, during which time she had steamed over two and a quarter million miles on line voyages and cruises.

PRINCIPAL PARTICULARS

	Himalaya	*Chusan*
Length Overall:	709ft	672ft 6in
Length B.P.	668ft	630ft
Breadth Moulded:	90ft 6in	85ft
Gross Tonnage:	27,954	24,000
Propulsion Machinery:	Both ships: Twin propellers driven by Parsons double-reduction steam turbines 34,000 SHP, 22 knots	
Passengers:		
First Class:	762	475
Tourist Class:	401	551
One Class:	1,416	N/A
Crew:	631	572

Acknowledgements: Mr W. 'Bill' Burrell, Sydney, Australia: Mr J. H. Buy, Eastleigh, Hampshire: Mr J. K. Byass, Bingley, Yorkshire: Mr John G. Callis, Deal, Kent: Mr Michael Cassar, Valletta, Malta: Captain J. L. Chapman, Helston, Cornwall: Mr J. G. Crawford, Cranleigh, Surrey: Mrs C. T. Dalgarro, Edzell, Scotland: Captain R. N. 'Dickie' Firth, Alverstoke, Hampshire: Captain Ian Gibb, P&O, London: Mr G. K. Godbold, France: Ambrose Greenway, London: Mr W. M. L. Hall, Leominster, Herefordshire: Mr P. Harris, Rotherham, S. Yorkshire: Mr R. W. Knight, Uckfield, Sussex: Mr I. F. MacFeegan, Bolsover, Derbyshire: Mrs H. 'Penny' MacLean, Morden, Surrey: Mr K. McCart, Greenfield, Bedfordshire: Mr B. Moody, Southampton, Hampshire: Helen Morgan, P&O's staff magazine, Wavelength, London: Mr N. D. Morris, Ilford, Essex: Dr M. Nicholls, Cambridge University Library: Mrs L. Palmer, P&O Group Information, London: Mr & Mrs N. Pound, Poulton-Le-Fylde, Lancashire: Mr B. Pudney, Yateley, Surrey: Mrs S. G. Quick, Sydney, Australia: Mr Stephen Rabson, P&O Group Information, London: Mr J. D. Sankey, Ulverstone, Cumbria: Mr F. R. Sherlock, Southampton: Mrs E. Simpson, Falkirk, Scotland: Mr D. Smedley, Potters Bar, Hertfordshire: Mr A. Smith, Paignton, Devon: Mr D. J. Stevens, Cooloongup, Western Australia: Public Relations Dept VSEL, Barrow-in-Furness, Cumbria: Public Relations Dept Vickers PLC, London: Mr E. L. Wentzell, Eltham, London: Roger Beacham and the staff at Cheltenham Reference Library: Finally to my wife Freda and to my two daughters Caroline and Louise:

Thanks also to the following who provided valuable photographs which are credited in the text and which readers can purchase as follows:

Mr R. R. Aspinall, Museum Of London, Museum In Docklands Project, Unit C4, Poplar Business Park, 10 Prestons Road, London E14 9RL.

Mr Ernest H. Cole, 46 Parkfield Avenue, North Harrow, Middlesex HA2 6NP.

Mr Alex Duncan, 14 South Hill Road, Gravesend, Kent DA12 1JN.

Mr Ian Spashett, FotoFlite, Littlestone Road, New Romney, Kent TN28 8LN.

Mr Don Smith, 7 Chapel Court, Hambleton, Selby, N Yorkshire Y08 9YF.

Other Titles From FAN PUBLICATIONS:

Famous British Liners Series:
Vol 1 SS *Oriana*-The Last Great Orient Liner £6.95
Vol 2 SS *Viceroy of India*-P&O's First Electric Cruise Liner £6.95
Vol 3 *Arcadia* & *Iberia*-P&O's Sisters For The 1950s £6.95
Vol 4 SS *Aquitania*-Cunard's Atlantic Lady £7.95
Vol 5 P&O's Five White Sisters-The *Strath* Liners Of The 1930s £12.95
British Warships:
HMS *Albion* - 1944-1973 The Old Grey Ghost £13.95

UK & European readers add £1.50 p&p: Other overseas readers add £3.50 towards air mail postage.

Write now for further details to:
FAN PUBLICATIONS
17 Wymans Lane
Cheltenham
Glos GL51 9QA
England
Fax & Tel: 01242 580290